Less Stuff, More Wealth
The End of Possession

Pierre Maarek

Warm thanks to Alyssa Glawe and Liana Wong for their valuable comments and corrections. Cover designed by Quentin Baes.

"Possession denotes the de facto claim on another entity based on exclusive access. If access is non-exclusive, the object in question is not being possessed. The concepts of possession and ownership often overlap, but are not the same. Ownership takes into account the entitlement to priority of access, which is based on agreements and other mutually consenting social protocols."

Wikipedia

Foreword

My father is a storyteller. I find interest in what he has to say; mostly because of the way he says it. He's a professor exactly like you would picture one. Curly grey hair that runs out of control and eyes that fill with excitement when he gets to the bottom of a question. He might be talking to himself as much as he is talking to you. But this is where his secret lies. As a child, he would tell me with excitement about the laws of physics and how the meridian of the Earth was measured with admirable precision 200 years ago. He would tell the same stories over and over again, and I would pretend that each time was the first.

Of course, I found it fascinating. But my father's splendid efforts to turn me into the next Delambre proved hopeless. Something less noble was distracting my attention. Something under my nose, on my feet: a pair of horrible sneakers that only children find attractive. They were cheap and yet so complex and well crafted. I knew no one able to make them from scratch with their own hands. And yet it seemed like buying them was the most trivial thing in the world. I felt almost guilty about it. In the early nineties, sport shoes were targets for campaigns against child labour: poor kids forced to make them on the other side of the planet. It all made perfect sense.

Adults should be careful with what they tell children. Young creatures can take things way too seriously—or maybe it was just me. My understanding was that the miracle of my sneakers was made possible due to sheer exploitation. At the time, the nations we now describe as "emerging" were still coined the "Third World". The concept of their take-off was nothing more than an unfulfilled promise. There was a sense—or so I felt—that the vast majority of the world population would be stuck in poverty till the end of time.

The fall of the colonial empires had been a disappointment. Development had never come. After all, wasn't this the reason why my father had left Tunisia, the country of his childhood? There he was, a survivor. I was one of the lucky few, born here in Western Europe. We were reminded of this fact every time something green and bitter had to be finished on the plate. Not to mention the benevolent school propaganda that France exceled at. It all made perfect sense.

The secret recipe behind the opulent wealth all around (cars, processed food... and shiny sneakers) was exploitation. My country was not rich despite there being poor ones. It was rich thanks to them. (Many people still hold this view.) A vast majority of mankind were sacrificing their lives in order to make our minuscule paradise possible. What a sad world! And yet, with the animal cruelty that children are capable of, I simply felt fortunate. Thank God I was born on the right side of the fence. It all made perfect sense.

Teenage time comes with its own torments. The spoiled kid I was had to wake up to the fact that our household had been living well beyond its means. Not only did we have no wealth, we were deep into debt. All the traveling and carefree ways of living had been paid for with future sweat. My parents had made the closest thing to a pact with the devil. And now was payback time.

The world suddenly felt more like a place to conquer than the Disneyland of my childhood. Financial difficulties made me stronger and I am immensely thankful for it. If my knowledgeable parents had been rubbish at dealing with their finances, at least I would learn from their mistakes! Little did I grasp at the time that I was given something vastly more valuable: an education.

My mother, an ardent feminist, was the opposite of possessive. She made sure that my upbringing was influenced by various surrogate parents and other environments. Some of the most useful things in life, I learned while staying with other families. It takes courage to acknowledge the limitations of your own parenting. And yet, putting your precious offspring in the hands of other—surely irresponsible—adults is the best thing you can do for them.

Apparently, I wasn't the only freak on the planet finding sport shoes more thrilling than rockets. At the age of 17, I fell in love with a subject that sounded anything but sexy: economics. We were so submerged in debt that during my first class, I found it bizarre that the professor would assume national savings to be a positive number. My definition of a well-off person was someone with no liability. Zero wealth was the objective!

This was the roaring first decade of the new millennium. The Asian crisis and the dotcom bubble, though recent, already seemed like distant memories. The future was full of promises. The long-awaited emergence of China and India was finally turning into a reality! Economics was a science after all. Soon, everyone would afford ugly sneakers. (Only the last assertion proved correct.)

As I reach my early thirties, these considerations are still at the centre of my life. Finance and data science are reshaping the world in astonishing ways. Sharing this passion is the motive behind the following pages. I like to say that *each one of us has only one story to tell*. I hope I can tell mine with the same talent and energy my father has. This book is dedicated to him.

Overview

The division of usage

Modern economics began with Adam Smith two hundred years ago. His achievement was less in the principles (or so-called "laws") than in the object. Smith focused on matters, which, at the time, were perceived as unworthy. What Alfred Marshall would describe a century later as the "ordinary business of life" has become the messy corpus of knowledge we know as economics. Welcome to a civilization where the trivial is offered a noble rank. Rocket scientists may deplore it (often rightly so). But mankind won't go back to the Moon before long. There simply isn't much for us there. We travel, read and socialize. In this day and age, good science is about improving people's lives. It is also the modest ambition of this essay.

From agriculture and craftsmanship, classical economics witnessed the rise of the first Industrial Revolution. It produced a complex organization of labour in which no individual alone could control nor understand the full picture (no matter what your boss thinks). The result was a world in which people produce far more than each of them would on their own. Such achievement was made possible by innovation—both technical and social. Institutions that enforce contracts were as critical as the steam engine. They range from democracy to double-entry bookkeeping. From the Ford Model T to today's smartphone, *division of labour* has been at the core of productivity gains. The early 20th century's second Industrial Revolution was about moving people to the city. In the process, land ownership ceased to be the natural store of value. But it was merely replaced by home ownership.

The current transformation is happening at the other end of the chain: a *division of usage*. What happened for production (the supply side) is making its way to consumption and investment (the demand side). Society has produced ever more while consuming in the same old way. Today, it is consumption itself that is becoming more complex. Once again, institutions and technology are driving the shift. It started with the ever-growing share of services over tangible goods. Health, art, entertainment, tourism, food: the vast majority of our consumption is now in the form of services. The tertiary sector represents close to 80% of the value added in the United States. In other words, it isn't much of a category anymore. It is becoming "the economy" itself. This process won't stop. The Information Age wants the remaining 20%.

John Lennon's "imagine no possessions" will become a reality, but not quite the type he had envisioned. In this world, *ownership* still exists as an institution. It is only *possession* (the stuff we keep in custody) that is being reduced to a bare minimum. The diagnostic is counterintuitive given the profusion of things that are produced on a daily basis. But it does not entail that less human-made objects must exist! Agriculture has become a tiny fraction of the economy while more crops are grown than ever before. It simply means that the way we coordinate usage is more intertwined. A system of consumption in which no one controls the full picture.

This transformation is not taking place because we are reaching a higher degree of wisdom (though this author hopes we are). It is not even happening because the protection of our environment makes it pressing. The division of usage is taking place because the Digital Age allows it. The gains that come with better resource allocation make us better-off—just like Adam Smith's division of labour.

Cloud investment

Farming families were able to provide for themselves through the possession of land and the physical assets that harvest it. Here we are now, urbanites dependent on the good will of grocery stores and restaurants. With the invention of the city, interdependence has allowed mankind to lift itself up. Despite the worries of survivalists and other paranoid types, reliance on others has been extremely beneficial. Institutions grown over centuries allow for the fruits of labour to be shared in a generally acceptable manner. Occasional bumps in the social contract are inevitable. They help steer the machine back in the right direction. Current debates around "the 1%" are an example. But it works. The cash in our pocket and the purely scriptural form we "own" on bank accounts are all social constructions that hold together because we choose to believe in them. Collectively.

In the 18th century, Physiocrats, like François Quesnay, considered that all wealth was derived from agriculture. The production of goods and services was seen as a mere transformation of the agricultural surplus. In essentially agrarian economies, this thinking was understandable. (Which makes you wonder how future economists—if they still exist—will judge our own paradigm.) In 1840, agriculture employed 70% of the labour force in the United States. In 2014, it represented barely more than 1% of Gross Domestic Product (GDP)! It is still essential by nature. But it simply isn't where value is created anymore. With great noise and social impact, industry has been following the same path. According to the World Bank, its share is now barely more than 20% of GDP.

Goods are turning into services. Car ownership is being replaced by mobility. Secondary homes are becoming holiday rentals. This transformation is well documented. But the implication on saving has received less attention. In both the developed and the emerging world, people still strive (with great difficulty) to purchase their home. Housing represents the largest share of the tradable assets owned by households. We will explain why giving up on *brick and mortar* is desirable and how it can be achieved. Millenials are already turning away from real estate, mostly because it has become unaffordable. This apparent curse is an opportunity.

If we are better off giving up on houses and tangible possessions, where are we supposed to store our nest egg? The vulgar topic of managing wealth should only occupy a tiny part of life. We will explain how *FinTech* (financial technology) makes smart investment simple, safe and cheap. Existing instruments are at an arm's reach. The reason why we are bad at dealing with money is not for lack of options. Quite the contrary! It is a lack of financial education combined with generally accepted beliefs. So let's start by questioning our assumptions.

Financial markets are a perilous place. No question about it. Most people wouldn't risk a dollar in these opaque machines. However, airplanes are equally obscure to us, and yet we risk our lives by using them regularly. We do it because we understand that we don't need to know everything about flying to benefit from airplanes. The same should hold for markets. Finance is a tool, not a cult. You do not need to immerse yourself in it. In fact, all you need to know is your limitations. Just like airplanes, there are a few things to understand before you can sit back, relax and enjoy the ride.

Die-hard mentality

I like my grandparents—though I never had a chance to meet them. My father's father was born at the turn of the 20th century. He was a Jewish Tunisian who worked for the *Banco Di Sicilia*. My own dad, who's a retired university professor, likes to joke that he is the "son of a banker, father of a banker". Like most bankers, my grandfather was terrible at managing his own finances. Like most professors, so is my dad. In fact, most of us (including this author) are terrible at building wealth. As Lao She's *Rickshaw Boy* states, our saving goals seem like a horizon we can never reach.

It won't come as a surprise that the best way to save more is to earn more. So let's not expect too much from frugality. The term "latte factor" was coined by David Bach to describe the unconscious spending on everyday things that do not add value to our lives (hence the reference to expensive coffees). His approach focuses on the gains that can be obtained from reducing small expenses. Reviewing our spending regularly is good practice. But it misses the big picture. Saving a few dollars a day (and alienating your friends in the process) won't do the trick. Your greatest asset is yourself. So if sipping coffee makes you happy, just go for it. (As Ethan Bloch puts bluntly: "Just have your f------ latte!")

Our ability to "think long-term" is part of what makes us human. And its drivers are complex. The

Stanford Marshmallow experiment was a research on delayed gratification led by Walter Mischel. It allowed children to choose between one cookie on the spot and two if they could wait for 15 minutes. The objective was to show that better self-control lead to greater success. (Sometimes, psychologists make economists look good.) Other studies focus on language. For example, Chinese would be associated with higher savings rates due to the absence of verb tenses. (What about the absence of a social security?) Again, let's put things in perspective. Protestantism, Confucianism, family values... Who knows? One thing is undeniable: saving is a tedious process. And we were not designed for boredom. This is why pension contributions are compulsory and why anyone who's not an accountant pays their taxes on the last day. Making saving fun is key to making saving possible in the first place.

Once we make more and save more, the investments we choose matter a great deal. Our intuition tends to underestimate the power of compounding. The development economist Angus Maddison reminds us that the United States became the United States by steadily growing at a mere 2% a year over the course of a couple of centuries. Granted, our lives do not last for two hundred years (yet). But next time you see this rate on a brochure, don't shrug your shoulders.

Whether you are a rigorous saver or a hedonistic consumer, the way you think about investments is probably not so different from my grandpa. Many aspects of your life would blow his mind, like flying around the world and accessing human knowledge from the palm of your hand. But your financial plans would sound boringly familiar to him: borrowing from a bank to pursue the dream of owning a home... If you have the soul of an adventurer, maybe you made a couple of stock market bets. Chances are you lost money in the process. Again, my grandpa saw all that in the Thirties. What then? Has progress ignored better investment methods? Of course not. Innovation offers new opportunities that we will explain later. For now, let's investigate why we think the way we think. Intuition and common sense are not absurd or irrational. But they are taken for granted.

Home, sweet home

Urbanisation is a recent trend. At the turn of the 20th century, 85% of the world population was still rural. The year when humanity became urban—with more people living in cities than in the country—was 2008! This long history weighs on us. The belief that land is the only reliable source of wealth is "planted" in our brain. Don't we call it "real" estate? In Medieval Europe, the term *property* essentially referred to land. Centuries later, we merely added buildings on top. As the economy grew more intricate, real estate came to embody a form of value we all comprehend and trust. Our natural aversion for complexity is what the French call "bon sens paysan" (the farmer's wisdom). It holds that anything we do not fully understand must be looked upon with suspicion.

Like most ancient things, *conventional wisdom* survived for a reason. It should not be ridiculed. Longevity is rarely coincidental. Suspicion is an insurance policy that protects us from erroneous decisions. Most things are too complex to be well understood anyway (including land). Distrust for the new is therefore a rational stance. The key is not to oppose conventional wisdom but to examine it. Like all insurances, it costs a *premium* (missed opportunities) in return for *protection* (preventing disasters). And like all insurances, it deserves a periodical review.

Brick and mortar

"How do our younger people see the future? They are not optimistic about housing. More than 40 per cent do not think they will ever be able to buy a flat. [...] There is also evidence of a reduced confidence in housing as an investment. More than half agree with the statement that "the housing market is too risky for ordinary people's investment". [...] So what do they want in terms of housing? They still aspire to property ownership even if they do not expect to be able to buy. Most see paying rent as a waste of money. And more than 80 per cent believe owning property is an essential symbol of being middle class. [...] The housing challenges facing young people in Hong Kong are not so unusual. In many cities around the world, new generations are finding it difficult if not impossible to get into home ownership. There are popular references to "generation rent" in countries such as Britain and Australia."

This article extract, based on a study by Ray Forrest and Yip Ngai-Ming, illustrates the situation in urban areas. It shows that the appeal of brick and mortar goes beyond rational economic thinking. Property is social status as much as it is investment. Supply and demand is probably the only "economic law" widely accepted. As the price of a good goes up, its demand should decrease because alternative options (assuming they exist) become relatively more appealing. What we see here is the opposite. Even when the alternative option (renting) is unaffected, an increase in housing prices makes ownership more desirable! The perception is that "paying rent is a waste of money".

The financial crisis of 2008 was a litany of Wall Street and British bank names going bankrupt and calling for outrageous government bailouts. But its root was planted deep into the housing market. Property was at the heart of the five preceding financial crises in developed countries. One reason is the sheer size of the thing. According to *The Economist*, world residential property in the rich world was estimated at around U.S.$52 trillion in 2011. Unless you are a macroeconomist, this number probably doesn't mean much to you. When twelve zeros come into play, the one figure you want to cling on to is World GDP (what "World Inc." produces each year). World GDP is around U.S.$70 trillion. U.S.$52 trillion is therefore a big number.

The figure is comparable to global stock market capitalization (the value of all listed companies). Is such high valuation reflecting the service rendered? The OECD, a think tank, estimates that households devoted an average 18% of their disposable income on housing. It represents a significant share of total spending. But so did food 50 years ago. The U.S. Department of Agriculture estimates that the average share of per capita income spent on food fell from 17.5% in 1960 to 9.6% in 2007! Will brick and mortar follow the same path? Possibly. At least, the necessity of eating did not prevent food from becoming cheap. The mere fact that "we need a home" is no guarantee that housing services will remain expensive.

It is no wonder real estate was involved in large financial crises. Subprime mortgages were nothing more than the expression of the notion that "everyone should own their home". Politicians, bankers, and the larger public all buy into this idea. People must own the roof above their head at all cost. (It's never good when anything is done "at all cost". By design, economists are the only species resisting this lure. It might be their only contribution to this world.) Our minds easily shift from the laudable "everyone should have a home" to the unreasonable "everyone should own a home". The fact that everyone should have enough food on their plate doesn't mean we should all own a plot of land.

Safe havens

No matter what, housing is perceived as the safest asset. A Fannie Mae survey done in 2011 showed that two-thirds of people saw homeownership as the safest investment after savings accounts. Housing is the vehicle we are most familiar with. It is the only asset we trust because it is the only asset we know! In fact, we think we know it so well that we lean towards over-confidence. We behave like the man who lost his keys and looks for them around the lamppost because this is where he has visibility.

This is what the psychologist Daniel Kahneman calls WYSIATI ("What You See Is All There Is"). It describes a bias for the things we are most familiar with. Think about the last time a friend visited you from abroad. As you brought this person into your world, she kept drawing conclusions about your environment. Statements like: "People aren't friendly here. The taxi driver was so rude to me." "It rains a lot in this city. My week there was awful." We have all been this person. Human beings draw general conclusions from the information they have, no matter how limited.

Let's set aside the emotional appeal of homes and remember that they are, first and foremost, a utility. Let's distance ourselves from them like we distanced ourselves from "tin cans on wheels". Because houses are both an asset (stored value) and a good (a place we live in), they feel like hitting two birds with one stone. Cars also are both an asset (when we drive them to work) and a good (when we take them for a ride). Since cars are much less durable, they have turned into the symbol of conspicuous consumption. Rightly so. The demand for cars is changing into a demand for transportation services. Could the demand for homes turn into a demand for housing services?

Homeownership remains attractive for the same reason why demand for private cars remains high: we like to see and touch our possessions. When buying property, you are buying something—it is fun! Choosing the right place, refurbishing it, furnishing it. You are experiencing the thrill of consumption without the guilt. You're not really consuming (or so you like to think). You are investing! Saving is boring, so embodying it into something tangible is appealing.

A place to stand and a lever

Leverage is the act of borrowing in order to invest more than the initial capital. Let's assume that you made an appointment with your banker. She likes you because you are a good family man with U.S.$100k in your savings account. You explain that you have long-term plans. You would like to borrow half a million dollars in order to invest in the stock market. Your existing savings can be used as a collateral. What do you think her reaction will be? After making you repeat, chances are your banker will politely show you the exit. This is understandable. And yet, it is no different to what millions of households do when contracting a mortgage.

The leverage in this example is obviously dangerous. If the value of your asset goes lower than the money you owe, not only do you lose it all—you are in net debt! The same holds for property. By contracting a mortgage, you are emitting a bond (with fixed or variable future payments) in return for an asset. The bank does not care much if the value of your home goes down. As long as your revenue covers the instalments or the value of the home does not fall below what you owe, they are covered. What you bought is called *equity*. And you bought it with high leverage and no diversification.

Let's assume that your neighbour Antony asked his banker for the same financial arrangement. But he did it in the form of a housing mortgage. Needless to say, he was welcomed. Antony deposited U.S.$100k as a lump sum and borrowed half a million more to purchase a U.S.$600k apartment. He finds himself exposed to the value of a particular home in a particular neighbourhood of a particular city. His leverage ratio is 5, meaning that the amount he borrowed is 5 times greater than what he put in. As time goes by and the mortgage is repaid, this ratio goes down. It reaches zero on the (distant) day he finally owns the apartment. At present, a price decrease of 20% (=1/5) would bring Antony below sea level into what is called *negative equity* (a euphemism for deep trouble). His initial U.S.$100k would be wiped out.

If the price is halved, Antony holds an asset worth U.S.$300k against a liability of U.S.$500k. His net debt is U.S.$200k. It may sound like fiction but a 50% plunge in real estate prices happened in several cities in America and Southern Europe after 2006. The nation-wide Case-Shiller index dropped by more than 30% between 2005 and 2009. The more leverage injected into the system, the more dramatic price swings tend to be. During declines, people like Antony are forced to sell at the worst possible time, pushing prices even lower into a vicious circle. Conversely, a 10% increase (U.S.$60k) in Antony's property value would translate into an actual 60% return relative to the money he put in (U.S.$100k). Leverage acts as an amplifier in both good and bad circumstances.

Being an ostrich

What if Antony was to close his eyes, carry on paying his mortgage and ignore the deep trouble he finds himself into? After all, it is all "unrealised" as long as he doesn't sell the apartment. In fact, this is the approach most of us take. For this reason, the first sign of a housing market downturn is a fall—not in prices—but in the number of transactions. Sellers refuse to acknowledge reality until they have to take their loss. Spain is notorious for the share of owners currently facing this situation. Barely able to repay the mortgage, they choose to ignore the real value of the house they bought. The lack of feedback is what explains the common perception that real estate is safer. In behavioural finance, this is called the *ostrich effect*, after the common myth that the animal buries his head in the ground to avoid danger.

Feedback is a powerful thing. If well managed, it is a positive force that is at the core of the relative success of market economies. These highly complex systems constantly reassess their decisions through price signals. The result is a trial and error mechanism that acts as a compass. In finance, the notion of feedback is called *mark-to-market*. Originated from accounting, it refers to the reporting of the value of assets at market price. In this case, it means confronting the opinion you formed to that of the rest of the world. People like to boast about how expensive apartments in the same area have sold for. But the truth is that they do not know the value of their asset until they actually sell it. Properties are heterogeneous and illiquid. Maybe the neighbour was able to obtain a good price because he gave himself time to attract a high bidder. What if you don't have this luxury?

Too much feedback is annoying. Think about the last time anyone commented on your weight gain. Instead of being thankful for the informative feedback, you felt irritated. No matter how much we want to believe we can learn from others, the ostrich in us just wants to be left alone. After all, we are not machines looking for constant improvement. Losing ourselves is pleasant, which is why alcohol and romance have been around for so long. What's so great about "truth", anyway? The difficulty to assess value is a shortcoming of real estate. Yet it turns into a desirable feature. When you own a stock, not only do you know its price precisely, yet still it is thrown in your face every single day! Mainstream media is constantly updating everyone about it (and for a reason this author fails to grasp). Constant feedback is unnerving. When the value of everything you own shrinks 10% in a day, you wish you could bury your head in the sand. Financial news feels very different when you have *skin in the game.*

Even when restricted to the field of economics, *value* is a controversial concept. It generally refers to "the maximum amount of money an actor is willing to pay". Think of it as an auction price. The next unit will go to the highest bidder, and his offer is what we call the current value. Excessive exuberance or despair can't be ruled out. Market prices are by no means perfect. But they are still the best we have to assess the value of tradable assets. We will get back to this. What matters for now is the perception it delivers. If valuations were taking place only once a year, stock markets would look way less wobbly. 10%

drawdowns would go unnoticed unless they proved enduring. That is to say that *perceived volatility* would be much lower. Unfortunately, we cannot avoid making eye contact with screens for a year. (Wouldn't it be nice?) What we can do is appreciate the shortcomings of our perception.

Walls all around

Physical real estate gives little flexibility. You might be willing to invest U.S.$100k into your asset. Yet you can't buy part of a house or apartment. It's all or nothing! Couples with children living in thriving cities face the exorbitant price of three-bedroom apartments. What if they wished to purchase half of it and pay a rent on the other half? Rigidity pushes leverage ratios up, no matter what the initial intention was. The same goes with the (First World) problem of investing in a second property. It often generates unnecessary risk. Here you are, back with a brand-new mortgage, exposing yourself to "deep trouble". All of it just because you had an extra U.S.$50k to invest.

Buying or selling is prone to high fees and long procedures. Any change in your personal situation is a risk for additional costs. A fixed rate of saving is forced upon you for the extremely long duration of the mortgage. Housing downturns typically occur when interest rates hike or challenging economic times drive out the most fragile owners. Those who can barely cope with monthly instalments find themselves forced to sell the entire asset. Due to crowding effects, these emergency exit situations happen at unfavourable prices. Liquidity concerns exist on all markets; but the lack of scalability of physical real estate leaves no middle way.

Another source of risk is the selection of the home itself. Granted, it can be fun. But what if you make a poor decision? If you dismiss this aspect, you are probably prone (like most of us) to what social psychology calls *illusory superiority*. This is the cognitive bias that causes most people to consistently overestimate their abilities and qualities relative to others. It is also referred to as the *above average effect*. The existence of this bias is one of the few things statisticians can prove. All researchers need to do is ask a sample of people to rate themselves against the rest. Justin Kruger and David Dunning demonstrated it in a 1999 paper titled *Unskilled and Unaware of It: How Difficulties in Recognizing One's Own Incompetence Lead to Inflated Self-Assessments*. They assigned tasks to a large group of participants, ranging from logic problems to assessing sense of humour. Each was ranked into four groups based on their results. When asked to assess themselves, all four groups estimated their performance to be above average. In what has come to be known as the Dunning-Kruger effect, the authors argue that the lowest-scoring people are precisely those who are less able to rate themselves! Lack of knowledge is compensated by a surplus of certitude.

Remember the poorly informed opinions you bitterly defended as a teenager? Meanwhile, your aunt Sarah, a recognised biologist, explained that modern science understands little about the functioning of the blood cell. As John Wheeler puts beautifully, "as our island of knowledge grows, so does the shore of our ignorance". Experts are also notorious for overestimating their own ability. In *Expert Political Judgment*, Philip Tetlock kept track of thousands of expert predictions. He collected them in different fields over a period of 20 years, guaranteeing anonymity. His conclusion was striking: experts were only slightly more accurate than chance and actually worse than a simple extrapolation algorithm.

The ownership paradox

Mobility is an asset. This is one of the most overlooked aspects in decision-making. The ability to move cheaply if need be is extremely valuable. The political mythology of the "country of homeowners" explains how becoming a stakeholder makes one a trustworthy member of the community. Not to mention the truism that being rich is better than being poor. But what does cold-blooded data say? Let's play a game. The following country ranking is based on a criterion that you must guess. Top ten (with more than 86%) are Romania, Lithuania, Hungary, Singapore, Slovakia, China, Croatia, Bulgaria and India. At the bottom of the list are Switzerland, Germany, South Korea, Austria, Turkey, Japan, France, Denmark, New Zealand and The United States. No, these are not infant mortality figures. These are homeownership rates.

Why do wealthier countries display lower rates? Isn't the opposite true for people? This ranking seems counterintuitive. But sometimes, using the part to understand the whole is a terrible mistake. At the country level, propensity to own one's home is inversely proportional to economic development. This observation is not absurd. The main feature of developed economies is the far-reaching interdependence between agents. Instead of baking their own bread and owning their own house, people specialize at what they do best and exchange the fruit of their labour in well-functioning markets. Granted, this vision is simplistic. But if you had to describe development in 140 characters, it would do the trick.

Advanced economies tend to better allocate resources by separating the usage from the ownership. Societies where entrepreneurs can only be the initial owners of capital fail to deliver the same level of progress (hello finance!). And less homeownership means more mobility. Professionals can move cheaply to locations that offer better opportunities.

As always, things are more complex. If correlation could replace theory, statisticians would rule the world. Causation can go both ways. Maybe good contract enforcement in advanced economies reduces the risk of entering rental transactions. Which would partly explain the data. Our point is not to prove that reducing homeownership rates is a good policy. Our point is to show that "a country of renters" is no impediment to economic development.

Financial equivalence

Let's go back to our thought experiment and assume that your request to the bank was accepted. You are now the delighted holder of a U.S.$600k equity portfolio, of which U.S.$500k is in borrowed money (just like Antony). Notwithstanding the hazardous nature of this leverage, you are left with a range of options. The first one is to replicate the position that Antony has achieved. He acquired a physical house while you are restricted to securities. Still, you could invest the whole amount in Real-Estate Investment Trusts (REITs), and maintain your renter status. REITs are simply companies that own income-producing real estate. They pay out dividends to their shareholders and can be publicly traded on major exchanges, like stocks. In other words, REITs provide investors with a liquid stake in property. It sounds complex because the concept is unfamiliar. But as a matter of fact, it is way simpler to purchase than physical real estate!

Many of the mentioned caveats are avoided. Your precious mobility is preserved. The (underestimated) time spent fixing natural wear and tear is freed up for more pleasant activities. Maintenance cost is indeed charged back to you and weighs on the REIT return. But these companies are professionals who manage such expenditures better than you would. The same goes for transaction fees and hefty procedures. In other words, net return is no lower than physical ownership. In addition to this, you have control over the amount invested, almost to the dollar. Saving a little each month helps segment your entry points. *Market risk* (buying at the wrong time) is thereby alleviated. *Selection risk* is also mitigated because your fund is based on a large pool of properties. *Liquidity* is higher since you can decide to sell any fraction of your asset at any point in time for a transaction fee lower than what Antony would pay to sell his property. The money would be available within days. Not to mention that Antony cannot choose to sell 5% of his apartment.

What does Antony have that you don't? Oh yes, he can touch it. He can say, "this is mine" with a flicker of pride in the voice. All you can do is contemplate the rather odd notion that you own a tiny fraction of hundreds of buildings! In other words, you lost *tangible possession*. Everything you own is embodied in no more than numbers on a screen… At this point, you realise that you would not want to invest the full U.S.$600k into those REITs. First of all, you appreciate that the leverage is unreasonable. Secondly, you realise that it makes little sense to put all your nest egg in residential property. Why not include commercial real estate in order to diversify? Why not other cities? Why not other countries? Why not other sectors? The decision Antony made is not as obvious as it first seemed.

O Capital! My Capital!

Material possession is the promise of eternity. Like all promises, we choose to ignore that it won't be fulfilled. Imagine for a moment that the billionaire Warren Buffet was given a chance to swap his shoes for those of an average twenty-year old man. Do you think he'd refuse? Is being rich really better than being young? Like Shakespeare's Richard III, Buffet would give "his kingdom" for time. Oscar Wilde expressed it beautifully in *The Picture of Dorian Gray*: "Youth is the only thing worth having. [...] I am jealous of everything whose beauty does not die. I am jealous of the portrait you have painted of me. Why should it keep what I must lose?"

This is mine

On the mind of Chinese men is the possession of a home. On the mind of Chinese women is the possession of a man in possession of a home. Which is why the possession of a home is on the mind of Chinese men in the first place. (Eventually, all you need is love.) Western societies aren't any different. They are merely better at concealing it. The urge to possess things is a universal human trait. We are evolved primates. Drawing a line and saying, "this is mine" is a way we offer a secure environment for our offspring and put our mind at ease. The instinct to possess is as embedded as our survival instinct. It takes a lot of will to resist it.

Many strive to emulate external signs of wealth and it usually doesn't end well. This is what economists (who have a passion for branding trivial concepts) call "signalling". Signals are meant to prove certain qualities because only those who possess the qualities are able to produce the signal. A good example is the diploma. Your next employer doesn't really care about the knowledge you acquired in your Philosophy class. But a degree on your resume tells that someone else has made sure you know how to think. A more cynical version would be, "I am from a stable household, educated and affluent enough to afford a degree in Humanities that bears no practical use. Therefore, I am well-groomed and educated." Agreed, this is pushing it. But when was the last time you sent a signal? I'd be surprised if it were more than one day ago.

We are sensual beings, highly sensitive to day-to-day experiences. It is more natural to attach value to houses, cars and jewellery rather than assets based on paper and on social norms. (Never mind that private property is a social norm in the first place.) Not to mention even less tangible forms of capital. Objects appeal to our backbone when the rest requires our brain. Therefore, physical assets "trade at a premium". It means that people are happy to pay slightly more for these things—a "sense-of-touch tax", so to speak. It is a general rule that you gain from deviating from the rest of the crowd.

Crowds are very good at avoiding *great mistakes* and terrible at making *great decisions*. You always distance yourself from them at your own risk.

Crowds are far from stupid: they are the paragons of conventional wisdom. In *Wisdom of Crowds,* James Surowiecki emphasizes the power of information aggregation in groups, when compared to individual (even expert) intelligence. His opening example shows how a crowd at a country fair was able to accurately guess the weight of an ox better than each individual in it. The success of user-generated content models like TripAdvisor, as opposed to traditional travel guides, illustrates the power of crowd knowledge in decision-making. But if you were to make all decisions according to the average person's opinion, you would be... average. There is nothing wrong with that, but it simply means you are avoiding both great mistakes and great decisions.

Everyone mistrusts bankers. Even bankers mistrust bankers (including this author). The sentiment that merchants of all kinds are parasites is deep-rooted. Our aversion against finance and commerce is part of our collective conventional wisdom. We wonder how people who make a living of "buying low and selling high" can be of any social utility. How could they not be toxic? Inherited instincts deserve respect. There is a reason why they survived. Refusing what we don't understand protects us from scams and helps avoid great mistakes.

The success of merchants has two rival explanations. The first is that mutual support and influence on the powerful allowed an elite to seek a rent on the rest of society. The old anti-Semitic tradition falls into this narrative. The second explanation is that merchants and intermediaries are actually useful, despite the fact that we don't intuitively comprehend what they produce. The rise of Venice, London, Hong Kong or New York was mainly driven by merchant activities.

Asset goods versus good assets

Something you save is something you don't enjoy immediately. It could be as diverse as a coin or a shampoo sample "borrowed" from a hotel. These things become assets. They are a reserve of energy you can keep for later. Once you use them, they turn into goods or services. Goods are often a form of value storage. A book provides no use until you read it. The point is that assets provide future gratification; something economists call *utility*. The concept of utility goes back to the 18th century, British philosopher Jeremy Bentham. The fundamental axiom of his political thinking was that "the greatest happiness of the greatest number is the measure of right and wrong". Don't deride it. This principle put him on the right side of history for most the great battles that were to come (slavery, rights for women and children and so forth). The point is that capital is only attractive to you, because it can eventually be turned into utility.

Note that the line between goods and assets is thin. Their definitions are not intrinsic qualities, but rather depend on the function. A common example is a car. If you use it to deliver mail, it is an asset. The same car, used for a Sunday ride, is now a consumed good. The latter usage produces utility while the former is an input for another production (mail delivery services). In this sense, let's call the car an "asset good".

We like instantaneous gratification. Our inclination for potential future utility is a painful thought process, with two consequences: first, it makes saving hard; and second, it favours assets that are also goods over forms of capital that do not deliver a *here and now*. We prefer our savings to be embodied in jewellery or real estate that we can admire. We are creatures of beauty, not optimization machines. Anything is preferable to a sequence of zeros and ones on a hard drive. In other words, we favour assets that deliver some utility now, even though we formally acquire them for the sole purpose of future utility.

Not being perfectly rational is part of the charm of being human. But there are better ways to be irrational than accumulating stuff. Not only is this model collectively unsustainable. It is costly! The urge to possess beautiful things blinds us to the core quality of an asset: the production of value. We fall for "asset goods" rather than good assets. What if none of your wealth was to ever be materialized into anything tangible?

Most capital is immaterial

In *Triumph of the City*, Edward Glaeser explores the impact of an underappreciated human invention. Cities are fantastic hubs for the circulation of ideas. Their complex interdependence acts as a wealth booster for the people who live in them. They make the sum greater than the parts. The author estimates that, "Americans who live in metropolitan areas with more than a million residents are, on average, more than 50% more productive than Americans who live in smaller metropolitan areas." Of course, such figures must be taken with a grain of salt. The crowd living in large cities is different from those of smaller agglomerations. But the scale effect still exists.

Pierre Philippes Combes and Laurent Gobillon quantify it in *The Empirics of Agglomeration Economies.* In the developed world, doubling the size of a city increases productivity by as much as 5%. In emerging countries, the figure is even greater. Reasons for this include economies of scale (infrastructure, universities, etc.) as well as proximity to larger markets and pools of know-how—in one word, access. Individuals gain what the Indian economist Amartya Sen defines as "capability", which is the opportunity to achieve the kind of life they value. (The capability approach aims at offering an alternative to utilitarianism.) Future potential benefit is precisely what capital is all about. In this sense, living in a large city is a form of asset. Note how diverse capital can be! We are far from the machinery or estate form that first comes to mind.

Capital can be even less palpable. In *Why Nations Fail*, James A. Robinson and Daron Acemoğlu trace the central role played by institutions in determining a country's circumstances. Ingenuity is everywhere at the base of society. Rigid systems that don't let initiative emerge—and don't cultivate it—are bound to fail. Good institutions left by history are worth way more than all the gold and oil in the world. As the Arab Spring shows, overruling past order and replacing it with desirable institutions is easier said than done. Models are competing and the rise of China is challenging the West's answer to development. But Rule of Law, respect of property rights and shared opportunities, still has common attributes of all advanced nations. Following the 1997 Hong Kong handover, China agreed to leave the city's institutions untouched for a period of fifty years. It didn't do so because it was forced to. It did so because Deng Xiaoping understood the value of British institutions in the territory. You don't kill the goose that lays the golden eggs.

Measuring the value of this type of capital is a challenge. What price tag do you put on the *capability* brought by being born in the United States as opposed to, say, being born in Liberia? What about the cultural heritage of being born in a multi-millennium culture? Surely, the wisdom (and culinary heritage) that it provides is worth something! We don't need to go this far to demonstrate the value of immaterial assets with hard figures. Thomas Piketty reminds us that even if we stick to companies' stocks (a "narrow" form of capital), the vast majority of market capitalization is already constituted of the immaterial type. Apple is not the most valuable company in the world thanks to the walls of its Cupertino headquarters. (They are actually quite ugly, which attests that humility pays off.) What's worth hundreds of billions of dollars is not even the intellectual property it currently owns in the form of patents. It is the potential ideas of its current and future employees—some of them not even born yet—and the way the company's culture is expected to harvest them.

A vast share of the capital that individuals own is invisible to the naked eye. It does not even show up on a hard drive. It lingers in a form that economists call *human capital*. This form of capital makes medical students (who eat canned food all day) somehow already "wealthier" than most young men with decent jobs. The former have not yet cashed out the dividends of their endeavours. But these can be valued today. In the fantasy world of financial theory, these students could borrow money now in order to start enjoying a comfortable lifestyle—something called the *lifecycle*. Outside the sick mind of economists, nobody does this. Students ride bicycles and get laid. But the thought experiment is forceful.

You are your most valuable asset

My mother often torments me with that she was unable to build any material wealth to be passed on. "Not being able to leave any inheritance for you, my only son, is one of my major regrets." I would reply to her that having been educated in a loving household by parents who donated cultural capital is worth way more! She thinks I'm simply being nice. I had a similar discussion with a friend who was desperately trying to purchase a studio flat she couldn't afford in order to "leave something behind" for her 12-year old son. The boy was raised in a stable and stimulating environment, with more books than the walls could fit and enough money to be comfortable and sufficiently little of it to understand its value. The notion that impalpable human capital is immensely worthy is counterintuitive. We have a hard time accepting the wealth we can't see.

Note that, quite unfairly, human capital heritage escapes any sort of taxation! Given its growing importance in our so-called "knowledge economy", it constitutes a major policy challenge. How can we sustain meritocracy in a world where most wealth is passed on through trivial aspects of daily life? Obviously, school is the key, but the task is immense. To make things worse, "assortative matting" is on the rise. Successful men marry successful women, adding to household inequality to an extent unseen before. An unintended consequence of the hard-won (and continuing) fight for gender equality! One virtue of the old (and unfair) system was to mate men with less affluent wives. Of course, there is no going back and society must find new solutions.

Human capital is way more than an intellectual gadget. Nurturing it is critical when dealing with one's own education and career choices. "What am I learning in this job?" is a matter at least as important as the figure on the paycheck. Unless you are Picasso's granddaughter, human capital is probably the most valuable thing you own. It has no price tag. But skyrocketing tuition fees in renowned universities are a reminder that its value is real. A study ran by PayScale, a research firm, has tried to look at the return on investment of education for several college degrees in America. The result was a mixed picture in which (unsurprisingly), best-known colleges and more technical subjects had a higher payoff. Overall, education is still a no brainer. It is the best and easiest investment decision one can make in life (not to mention the personal pleasure and accomplishment). Good schools are very much aware of it. They won't let it be the bargain it used to be.

You might assume that human capital can only increase over time. But as many seniors learn the hard way, experience can turn into an unlikely burden (at least in the eyes of employers). Human capital is an ability to produce economic value. It is defined as a stock of knowledge, experience, habits, motivation, creativity, etc. As such, it reaches a peak at some point. There is no age to great accomplishment. But there comes a point where human capital won't feed you, even if you've accumulated an encyclopaedic knowledge of good jokes. It is therefore reasonable to set aside some of the fruits of your labour for the future.

I personally dislike the dull vision that saving is about helping your future self pee straight and feed himself. Incontinence management is not an exciting project. No wonder people save so little! First, as naive as it may sound, we should trust our children. Future society is likely to be better than today's in most ways. Care for the elderly has no reason to fade. The perception that new generations are worse at taking care of their old is misguided. People are less likely to keep parents inside their homes, which does lead to solitude for the aged. But transfers between generations have simply become institutionalized through retirement schemes. The time when children used to be a form of investment is long gone. Another reason for embracing a positive view of saving is that it represents more than retirement. It is extra freedom. Most of us are slaves to the money, one way or another. Working is in our genes and we love it. But it sucks that we have to. Whatever you make of it, saving means more options.

In banking, I always felt astonished at the "money problems" of my co-workers. They sound similar to those of ordinary working class people: high incompressible spending relative to income and frustration with what they can't afford. Of course, their issues are not as serious. But I naively expected the top 1% of the income bracket to have no money problems! In the household I grew up in, "wealth" meant the ability to pay bills on time. Consumption loans were my first encounter with interest rates and the power of compounding. As too many families know, if saving is hard, repaying debt is way worse. The "money problems" of my privileged colleagues is a reminder that human beings need unreachable horizons to keep walking.

After adjusting their lifestyle to more income, people find little extra enjoyment. For example, they would gradually take restaurants for granted. Add to this that humans compare themselves to the neighbour and not to the average person! Making more money means moving to better neighbourhoods, surrounded by wealthier people. Back to square one. All that matters is to make more than your brother-in-law. Two Nobel Prize laureates, Angus Deaton and Daniel Kahneman, conducted a study on money and happiness. It analysed Gallup surveys of 450,000 Americans in 2008 and 2009. The conclusion was that money brought two forms of happiness: a day-to-day contentment and an overall "life assessment". If the latter kept increasing with income, there seemed to be a strong cap on the former. Day-to-day wellbeing reached a plateau at U.S.$75,000 a year. If money comes your way, this raises the case for saving as opposed to changing your lifestyle drastically. Buy yourself extra time, freedom and peace of mind.

The case for equities

Let's put things into perspective, both in space and time. (Apologies for the avalanche of numbers.) The following figures are all in trillions of U.S. dollars. In 2013, the United States GDP was 17. This figure is what "America Inc." produced in a year. It is therefore a *flow*, like a salary. The *stock* is the wealth held by America's households. It is the sum of their assets such as property, 401(k) and other financial holdings, minus the sum of their debts such as mortgages, car loans, credit cards and student loans. According to a Pew Research Centre analysis of Census Bureau data, this stock reached 40 in 2011.

Including human capital, the United Nations estimates total wealth in the U.S. in 2008 to be 118. Though a wild guess, it illustrates once again that America's asset is mostly its people and institutions. For now, let's focus on homes versus companies.

Zillow, a research firm, estimates that at the end of 2013, the combined value of U.S. homes topped 25. Meanwhile, the value of companies listed in the U.S. was approximately 19. Real estate is therefore one of the main forms of wealth for American families. No wonder it is perceived as rock solid. But let's add time to this macro picture. How did we get there?

Economists Karl Case and Robert Shiller calculated the home price index back to 1890. Their work has led to what is now known as the Standard & Poor's Case–Shiller Home Price Index. Few countries outside of the United States possess such long reliable records. In *Irrational Exuberance*, Shiller unravels a popular myth. Contrary to widespread perception, the value of American homes has produced very modest returns since 1890. In real terms, it achieves less than 1% per year! After a strong increase at the end of the nineties and a subsequent collapse, prices in constant dollars were still a meagre 20% higher than where they were more than a century ago.

In the meantime, stock indexes have increased dramatically. In *Houses vs. Stocks: Who Wins the Long-Run 'Sharpe' Race?*, Jose Ursua goes back to the same year for a series of developed countries (Australia, Canada, Finland, France, Iceland, Japan, Netherlands, Norway, Spain, UK, and U.S.). He estimates that the average yearly return of housing was 1.7%. For stocks, it was 5.6%, which is equivalent to a doubling in real terms over periods of approximately 12 years.

This is possibly the most underappreciated fact in personal finance. Trumped by inflation and anecdotal evidence, our intuition fails to detect that real estate delivers poor returns in constant dollar terms. Why can't we see it? One reason is that housing is the only asset we are truly familiar with. People do keep track of the nominal value of the family home over thirty years. Even at such slow rates, the price tag would have doubled over the period. And maintaining a positive real return over the long run isn't bad! Sheltering from inflation is already something. Gold is the typical example of an asset that has shown no return in real terms from 1800 to 2000. And yet it is (wrongly) perceived as a valid option.

Financial assets feel inconsequential because they leave no trace. In the absence of an *anchoring*, their solidity is understated. We (understandably) do not pay attention to the value of stock indexes. No one, besides disturbed geeks, would remember the value of the S&P500 index twenty years ago. What we remember is epic bankruptcies! Dramatic stories that capture the imagination. We miss the silent and gradual success of the majority. Next time you hear about an index trading at 2000 points, remember that its inception level was probably 100.

The irony is that most of the savings people own are already immaterial. They exist in entitlements to retirement plans. You can't sell those rights to someone for hundreds of thousands of dollars. Yet they are worth this much. Their value is simply implicit. People focus on the house they own (and haven't finished paying) when their true wealth lies in boring rights accumulated over decades.

Traveling light

Have you ever felt the exquisite pleasure of traveling light? In the world of investment, mobility and low maintenance are underappreciated. What makes housing bubble busts so devastating is the long deleveraging that follows. Getting rid of the vast amounts of debts they incur takes time. Mobility is the first thing families lose during a housing crisis. It strongly impedes subsequent recoveries. People can't move until they have repaid large chunks of debt or the housing market recovers. Predictably, places with jobs are hit less hard. Households who bought homes in Manhattan or San Francisco were relatively sheltered from the storm. Those in the wrong locations, like Detroit, faced the double punishment of greater financial loss while being trapped in areas with higher unemployment.

The history of mankind is evolution from nomadism to sedentism. A change that took place around 12,000 BC. Gains in productivity allowed engaging in more than mere survival. Moving from a society of hunters-gatherers to one of agriculture and breeding has not only increased yields. It unleashed new resources that could be used for new activities. These have grown into most of the jobs we know today. Sedentism opened the way for urbanisation. Cities allowed ideas, best practices and people to circulate. In a sense, they made us nomads again within a sedentary environment.

As the process continues, it reaches new corners of our lives. This isn't about communication technology making distances irrelevant, or about people working from home. Location matters and proximity is key for collaboration. If anything, large metropolises are gaining momentum. Witness the importance of financial and technological hubs. The new nomadism is the ability to move from one city to the next at low cost. It is about going to where opportunities flourish and our skills are most valued. This mobility is strengthened by the prevalence of the English language and the globalisation of culture (whether we like it or not). The illiquid nature of land and real estate impedes circulation. It turns accumulation of capital into a burden to be dragged. What the city accomplishes for our work, finance does for our wealth. Digitalization and better contract enforcement means that managing complex cross liabilities is cheaper than ever.

Myths worth busting

It is assumed that financial markets are fit for three types of individuals. The first is the rich who can afford the expensive entry ticket and high management fees. The second is the reckless gambler. The third is the talented individual who "knows his stuff" and makes a living by trading from home. This is wrong. The first type was the norm in the previous century. The second type is no role model. And the third one only exists in TV commercials for brokerage firms. Modern finance is for everyone. It is an answer to inefficient accumulation and the need for mobility. Before I explain why, let's deconstruct some of the popular myths that turn good family men into maniacs.

Time the market right

Wrong. My dad once told me an anecdote about his own father. He taught him that an important rule of thumb was to buy in falling markets and sell in rising ones. After a decade spent on trading floors, I think about my grandpa's advice with a smile. There is no secret way to trade at the right time. That is, buying before an increase and selling before a fall. Some firms do it for a living, with mixed success. But as an individual, you simply do not have the resources. Timing the market is a chimera, the modern version of alchemy. Just get over this obsession.

Many professional traders will persuade you (and themselves) that "knowing about the market" is necessary in order to buy and sell wisely. In any field, becoming an expert means obsessing with something that most people do not care about. Finance is no exception and market experts abound. The fact that some make a living out of it, leads the rest of us to miss the point. Our response, whether it is revulsion or fascination, is too emotional.

When buying a home, people do not try to time the market. They will look for the best bargain. But it is different from postponing their acquisition for several years. This form of heuristics is embodied in the popular notion that "any time is the best time to buy a home". Here is an example of beneficial *conventional wisdom*. People understand their limitation when it comes to timing the housing market. They would ignore this dimension and focus or other constraints (mortgage, family situation…) to motivate the moment of acquisition. Why do our brains behave differently when it comes to stocks?

I blame Warren Buffet, the delightful CEO of Berkshire Hathaway and most successful investor of the 20th century. To make his case worse, Buffet wrote numerous books that were supposed to share his trading secrets. Since I trust it wasn't for the money, such deeds must have been committed with good intensions. And hell is paved with good intentions. It feeds the popular belief that stock markets are about buying what is "cheap" and selling what is "expensive". This approach is not only illusory. It is damaging.

A zero sum game

Wrong. The concept is borrowed from game theory and describes a situation in which a participant's gain is balanced by the loss of others. Think of it as people sharing a pie. The specificity of *zero sum games* is that no matter what strategy participants go for, the size of this pie is fixed. Poker, heritage disputes and love triangles all fit the description. Stock markets do not. They contain an element of diverging views and the gains of some are the losses of others in the short term. But this is not the big picture. In the long run, the pie grows indefinitely because financial markets produce wealth. (Hard to believe, I know.)

Brokerage firms are feeding the zero sum game misconception. Their marketing target is the young adult male from the human species (a specimen full of hubris). Commercials typically feature a handsome young man who installed twelve computer screens and turned his living room into a NASA mission control centre. Perfectly shaved, he uses his skills to "sense the market" and make millions of dollars by trading at low fees. (You have to admire how much advertising can say in a few seconds.) Guess what, these companies are brokerage firms! Their income originates from the (arguably low) fees they charge on every transaction. They would endorse any story as long as the conclusion is that you must trade more. They want you to trade like Coca-Cola wants you to drink.

Wrong assumptions lead to wrong conclusions. From the zero sum game perspective, two options exist. The first is to fight this war. After all, playing a zero sum game isn't irrational if you think that you are better than average. (A belief shared by most.) Those who follow this route may waste a bit of money while having some fun. No worse than Disneyland. The second option is to stay away from the battlefield. Crowds are not stupid. So this is the preferred option of the vast majority. Except that markets are no battlefield and staying away from them won't make you better off.

Trading generates revenue

Wrong. Of all asset classes promoted by brokerage firms, the type I dislike the most is currencies. Stay away from it and cover the eyes of your children when passing by. The reason is simple: the expected gain from any investment comes from *exposure*. Allow me to insist: exposure, not trading. Currencies are the worst asset class because they leave no room for exposure gains (like the cash in your pocket). The foreign exchange market is an actual zero sum game!

Being *exposed* (or *holding a position*) means benefitting from a price move. Someone who owns Nestle shares is exposed to Nestle. They have a *long position* in the company. If the stock price goes up, so will the value of the investment. The opposite is called a *short position*. It benefits from a fall in the price. This concept is counterintuitive. But yes, it is possible to gain from a price fall. For more details on how it works, I recommend Michael Lewis' enjoyable book, *The Big Short*.

Trading is a cost. It is true for financial assets as any other type (real estate in particular). This cost includes commissions, taxes... and time. As someone whose job is to design trading algorithms for large asset managers who take their money seriously, I ask you to take my word for it. The objective is to reduce this cost. Trading is not a source of income. Making a living out of the act of buys in selling is the job of very specific people. An informative and entertaining introduction to this is another Michael Lewis book, *Flash Boys*.

To us mortals, trading is a necessary evil to achieve exposure. The notion that being active can be detrimental is not intuitive. Shouldn't "doing more" be better? The mistake is to believe that the revenue derived from investment is the counterparty for some work (in this case, trading). This isn't you selling your labour force! This is you providing access to your capital and putting it at risk. Just take it as a piece of exceptionally good news. You have extra time for more interesting stuff.

Pick the right horse

Wrong. Most individuals set their first foot in financial markets through the acquisition of the shares of a particular firm. Maybe their local branch manager suggested some "privileged" deal for a corporation going public. (This usually ends in court, years later.) Maybe it was a personal decision based on the attraction to a certain company, e.g. the appeal of owning a piece of Google or Tesla. After all, isn't it cool to put your faith in great entrepreneurs?

This approach is called *stock picking* and it makes total sense. But it is mistaken for the natural way to engage in share holding. Most *retail investors* (a polite name for "small guys") choose stock picking when they should not. Investors are like family men who buy the coupé instead of the minivan. Driving out of the dealership with a dull family car is not exciting. But function should come first. Stock picking is for risk takers willing to "play around" with part of their money. It is the smarter version of the casino gamble. (This time, the odds are in your favour.) But it simply isn't what reasonable people need. They need something boring and safe. They need the minivan.

This misunderstanding damages the reputation of stock markets because it occasionally annihilates hard-earned family savings! These personal tragedies are only the visible part of the iceberg, the *sunk cost*. (I know it's hard to feel sympathy for investors.) The most damaging effect lies beneath the surface, in what economists call *opportunity cost*. By driving reasonable households out of finance, misconceptions prevent the majority from benefitting.

Be prepared to lose it all

Wrong. The belief that one should only adventure in financial markets if he is ready to lose everything is a consequence of the stock picking fallacy. A given company can go burst or wipe out its equity holders. But the market as a whole is structurally different. The whole is more than the sum of its parts. In his insightful *Antifragile*, Nassim Nicholas Taleb notes that restaurants are a notoriously unstable business. Most fail over their first 3 years. But the restaurant industry as a whole is incredibly resilient. It has lasted for centuries without showing any sign of extinction. Owning a tiny piece of every single restaurant business on the planet wouldn't simply be safer than owning one—it would be an entirely different matter. The only threat you face now is large-scale annihilation of the entire industry. Say if (God forbid!) some new process makes eating irrelevant.

Good to know. But you simply cannot own a tiny piece of all the restaurants on the planet. Going around every single one, convincing the owner to sell you a share worth a fraction of a cent, collecting your due, ensuring you are not being conned... You would have to be a wizard! And wizards have better things to do than run restaurants. But here is where the magic of our complex economy kicks in. On a daily basis, we collectively achieve vastly more than as separate individuals. Likewise, we are capable of owning a tiny fraction of thousands of business on the planet.

There are valid concerns besides the fear to "lose it all". Even the most diversified asset is no guarantee against a tough ride. The prospect of losing half the value of one's investment is enough to draw people back to the shelter: brick and mortar. This reaction is understandable but misplaced. There is no reason to believe that a home is safer. When the subprime crisis began in August 2007, the Yale University economist Robert Shiller warned the Federal Reserve Board. "The examples we have of past cycles indicate that major declines in real home prices—even 50 percent declines in some places—are entirely possible going forward from today or from the not-too-distant future." And this doesn't even account for the effect of leverage! High levels of debt mean that a 10% slump is sufficient to wipe out someone's initial investment.

We explained that the absence of *mark-to-market* is a key reason for the false perception that housing is less volatile. Imagine that the value of your home was reassessed daily, and thrown at you on the media. One day, you would learn that its price is up 2% because a company has decided to establish an office nearby. The next day, it would fall 1% because your neighbour installed an ugly veranda. It sounds silly but, in a way, it is implicitly happening. You don't know the value of your home until you actually sell it. Financial markets aren't intrinsically riskier. The long-term behaviour of diversified indexes is rather benign. The trick is to blissfully ignore the daily noise they throw at you.

A recurring argument is that homes must be safer because, at least, you can live in them. Owning a shelter must be helpful when things go really bad. And I mean never-ever-seen sort of bad. Well, if things go wrong to the extent that most listed companies have become worthless; the polite social contract that makes your property inviolable is likely to blow up. (Expect the pitchforks to be at the gate!)

The notion that "housing is different" is a tale. Finance allows for a range of risk and return profiles. The equivalent of homeownership is simply one of them. It can be replicated. Nothing is inherently different about property besides the animalistic gratification of possession.

The only thing worth owning

The heuristics of *conventional wisdom* dictate that you should stay away from what you do not understand. Fair enough. So let's widen our understanding! You need to know more about finance before you can finally ignore it. This book is no lecture. But its objective is partly to empower. One thing this author has learned over the course of his own academic years is the importance of keeping it fun.

My proposition is that we should stop going after the things that defined the *good life* in the 20th century: a home, a car, and a vacation venue. But the end of possession is not the end of property. It is not even restrained consumption. So what can we replace these things with? Entitlements based on social protocols, recorded as computer bits in remote datacentres? Precisely. Not just because it sounds cool (though it does). We should do so because it is in our own best interest.

If intangible assets can improve our lives, we need to understand what they stand for. The first step is to go back to the concrete reality they mask. FinTech is only a distribution channel. Smart investment is not just for experts and professionals. Some key concepts are explored, hopefully in an entertaining manner. Narratives and thought experiments are preferred to jargon and formulas.

Source of wealth creation

Kyle Conroy, a student at the University of California, Berkeley imagined the following. Let's say that you are back in 1997. You are looking for a laptop and have set your eyes on Apple's best product at the time: the PowerBook G3 250. Life is short, so you decide to purchase the ground-breaking piece of technology for $5,700. Eighteen years later, in 2015, what is left of it is a clunky piece of plastic that flashes when you plug it. Something you could sell for ten dollars on eBay. You might have used the laptop to write Harry Potter, in which case you made a pretty good use of this asset. But chances are you did not. It helped you get familiar with this new thing called "the Internet" (a valuable learning experience). But let's face it; the cheaper alternative would have done the job just fine. Going for the top of the line was conspicuous consumption. What if instead of pouring this money into the Apple product, you had invested it in Apple shares? At today's valuation, you would be a millionaire.

Such exercise is deceitful and easy to design in retrospect. There was no way for you to guess that Apple would become the most valuable company in the world. It might as well have gone bankrupt. $5,700 was a decent amount of money back in 1997 and personal computers were still a luxury. Nevertheless, the merit of this thought experiment lies elsewhere. It is a striking illustration of *productive capital*. Again, your usage of the laptop did create value. But it compared poorly with the same amount spent on putting to work –commute and pencils included- the young Jonathan Ive (now Chief Design Officer at the company). Again, success stories are easy examples; but the point is that businesses in general are good at making capital productive. Let this anecdote act as a reminder next time you treat yourself with the next gadget.

Meet the cash flow

The only certain thing about stocks is that their prices *tend to go up*. To put it another way, the long-term return of businesses is positive. Some firms will go bust; others will flourish. But in the *long run* (whatever that means), money piled into the *typical company* (whatever that means) will be worth more than the same amount kept under the mattress (we know what that means). Cash is worth less over time than productive assets. This candid statement is no recipe for making a fortune. It simply implies that stock markets eventually beat their previous high. Prices will reach any given level above the current one after enough time.

How much time is "enough time"? How low can prices go before a new high is reached? These are valid questions. The economist John Maynard Keynes famously remarked, "In the long run we are all dead". Therefore, the knowledge that prices eventually recover is of little relief. Moreover, what do we mean by the *typical company*? Can I invest in it? As Henry Kissinger joked, "Who do I call if I want to reach

Europe?" The typical company exists no more than the average person. But there are proxies. For the moment, let's walk away with one key fact: preserving inflation-adjusted value over decades is already an achievement.

An asset is expected to generate a series of future revenues for its owner. These are called the *cash flow*. The name is ugly but graphic enough to strike the mind. Cash flows come in all shapes and profiles. Some are highly predictable; others are volatile. Valuation is the exercise of assessing how much one is willing to pay today (the *present value*) for being entitled to the future cash flow. That is all there is to it. Assets are much simpler than people, which is why mathematics is easier than psychology.

Are you willing to pay more for a reliable cash flow of $2 a year (asset A) or for a highly unpredictable one (asset B) that is expected to produce $3 a year? Think of asset B as that restaurant your brother-in-law just opened. $3 a year is what you expect from it but things could go wrong. Not so much with asset A, which may consist of U.S. Treasury Bills. If you are allergic to risk, maybe asset B has to promise $5 to become attractive. The price at which you are happy to buy the asset determines the rate of return that you expect from it. This is called the *yield*. For example, if you are willing to pay $100 for asset A, you are accepting a yield of 2%. If you are willing to pay the same for asset B, you are accepting a yield of 3%. Asset B is uncertain, which is why you are asking for a higher yield.

The notion of yield is everywhere in the world of investment. It may take different shapes but it is the ultimate yardstick of asset valuation. Think of it as comparing a year of rent payments to the value of the apartment. On the stock market, the most basic metric is the *price-earning ratio* ("PE" for friends). As the name states, it divides the price of a stock by the amount of earning that it entitles to. For example, I may hold a $40-stock from a company that earned $2 million over the last year. Since it has a million shares in circulation, each share entitles to $2. In this case, the *price-earning ratio* is 20 (=40/2). The yield is simply the inverse of this "PE". In other words, they describe the same thing. My PE of 20 is nothing more than a rough equivalent of a 5% (=1/20) yield. By investing $40 into this asset, I expect to receive $2 every year. The point is that despite their seemingly diverse nature, all assets speak the same language. An apartment and an IBM stock are not that different.

Another key notion is that finance deals with *assets* and *liabilities*. A liability is the mirror image of an asset. It is its counterparty. The cash in your pocket is an *asset* to you (though its yield is null). It is a *liability* for the rest of society; something they owe you collectively. Don't forget that money is simply another form of debt. Look at all the things that total strangers do for you every time you hand them this worthless piece of paper.

Buying versus renting

The most common financial fallacy is the popular notion that "paying rent is a waste of money". The reasoning is simple. When renting a place, you throw away money each month for the sake of pure usage. By borrowing and spending a little more each month, you could both live there and eventually possess the place. What makes real estate confusing is its dual nature: an asset and a final good. The ability to borrow to purchase it also adds to the complexity.

Future rents—net of costs and maintenance—are the *cash flow* that the house produces. It is all the value that this asset will ever generate. Given its expected level and the uncertainty around its evolution, the house is worth a certain amount. This price should be such that the rate of return (the yield) is reasonable.

For example, an apartment worth $1 million may have the sum of yearly rents adding up to 4% ($40,000). If the price were as high as $4 million, yearly rents would represent no more than 1% (a very low yield). The place would be "overvalued". That is to say that we would easily find another asset (X) with similar risk that yields more than 1%. Investing the $4 million in asset X and renting the apartment with the proceeds would be a preferable option.

Homeownership is therefore not an obvious decision. The reason for this is quite simple: a house is an asset like any other. It has a cash flow, a yield, a risk, etc. Banks happily lend large amounts of money to homebuyers. This adds an extra dimension to the problem, making comparison difficult. But *leverage* is merely an independent aspect that can be achieved on any asset. The fact that owning a home is preferable to not owning one does not mean that acquiring your home is preferable to renting it.

Businesses at the core

What differentiates a common good from an asset is the existence of a cash flow. This is why a banana is not an asset. A good delivers pleasure (utility) now. If I can expect more from it by deferring its usage, it turns into capital. It can be physical or immaterial. It can be reliable or highly uncertain. But it is capital nevertheless because I expect it to deliver something in the future. This is what differentiates the banana from the university degree.

The list of things that generate cash flow is not unlimited. One is your workforce. Another is land or real estate. Other examples include great works of art and patents. But the natural-born cash flow generator is the company. It is the main institution that our societies have invented to nurture a variety of *value added* activities. Put X in the box, and out comes X plus a little something. Sovereign countries might issue debt instruments that are a type of asset. But it eventually sits on the production of companies (through the collection of taxes). When one buys a bond issued by the U.S. Treasury, he is putting his trust in the stability of the institutions of the United States. But he is equally putting his trust in the means of production of American businesses. Value generation puts the company—public or private—at the centre of the picture.

A bond issued by a corporation rests on the back of the ability of the firm to generate the value that will repay the debt. Deeper into the core is the world of *equity*. Owning a fixed claim on future revenues is one thing. Owning a stake is another. In order to repay a debt of X, the business will need to generate at least X before maturity. Any gap with the objective (positive or negative) will be left to the owners of the business: equity holders. French politician Edouart Herriot famously said, "Culture is what is left in the mind when all has been forgotten". Well, *equity* is what is left in the company when all has been settled. It is the ultimate *skin in the game*, placing the investor not as the owner of a claim on the business, but as the owner of the business itself.

The invention of the public company

Owning a stake in a company is a complex thing. Let's go back to the restaurant that your brother-in-law is opening. Instead of borrowing the necessary funds, his plan is to sell *equity*. In other words, he wants to sell you a share of the business for an amount of money you deliver now. If the deal goes through, a given percentage of the profit will be yours indefinitely; for as long as you keep your share. Imagine the endless discussions with him about how much 1% of his restaurant should be worth. The place does not even exist yet, but there is a fierce disagreement between the two of you. He believes that his business is already worth a million dollars because the concept is innovative and the project already quite detailed. For this reason, he wants to charge you one hundred thousand dollars for a 10% stake!

You think that no one would pay such a large amount of money for what is essentially a risky bet. Your wife supports you. What if your brother-in-law marginally fiddles the figures? Wouldn't it be in his interest to lower the apparent profit the restaurant makes? You spend sleepless nights surfing the Internet searching for the legal structure that would best protect you as an investor. You even sought for advice from your friend Audrey, who happens to be a lawyer. But after wasting too much of her time, you feel bad. Not to mention that you'd rather maintain the *entente cordiale* (the peace agreement) within the family. This situation is getting pretty complicated. And yet this is the project of someone close to you! What if it was some random stranger? Owning a stake in someone else's business is definitely no simple thing.

One of the most formidable inventions of the 17th century is certainly the *public company*. The first trace of a corporation issuing shares for the greater public goes back to 1601. It was the Dutch East India Company. It formed under a royal charter that granted it a twenty-year monopoly on trade with the East Indies. The merchants would form a limited liability company. Investors would put money for voyages in return for a share of the profit if the trip was successful. Ironically, it was also involved in the first known market crash: the *tulip bulb craze*. In 1634, some of their ships carrying tulip bulbs set off a craze that resulted in the famous crash. A new world was born, with new possibilities and new risks.

A publicly held company is a corporation whose ownership is open to the general public. It is divided into shares that are freely tradable. For the company itself, the appeal is access to the capital it needs for its investments—money that sleeps in people's bank accounts, or more likely in their pension fund and insurance. For the public, the appeal lies in making idle resources productive. They have ideas, you have means. The logistics and legal complexity of such a system should not be underestimated. The "brother-in-law thought experiment" provides a glimpse into the potential conflicts of interests. The institutions that make the contract enforceable have been erected over centuries of trial and error.

Regarding the social added value of the public company, controversy exists. Some see it as the great evil of financial capitalism spreading its wings. This view should not be dismissed. The distance put between the final owner and the company's activity has drawbacks. It makes profit a more central measure of the overall "performance". To use a fashionable concept, *shareholders* stop being *stakeholders*. When you own part of your brother-in-law's restaurant, you care about the quality of the food he produces, as well as the working environment he provides. You would hate feeling responsible for harming your clients' health or for poor employment conditions. In other words, profitability is not the only metric you use to assess the quality of your business. As a distant investor possessing a fraction of a multinational, you feel less accountable.

In psychology, this is illustrated by the Milgram experiment. It turns average people into torturers by simply adding distance between them and the person they are brutalizing. A scientific authority asks them to send electric shocks to distant subjects for the sake of a supposed experiment. They are told to send the shock every time the subject gets the answer to some question wrong. Of course the so-called "subject" is an accomplice. The actual subjects of this experiment are the people sending the shocks. They can hear the accomplice scream and beg for mercy after a series of increasing voltage. An important aspect is that they cannot see them and believe they can't be seen either. When the "scientific authority" (basically some guy with a white coat) tells them to carry on and ignore the screams, an appallingly large majority of the people proceed. Comparing this to financial capitalism is a little brutal. But it illustrates that we behave differently when distance is put between us and the consequences of our actions.

What keeps things for turning inhumane in the public company is a series of institutions built over centuries. There are intermediaries between merciless investors and exposed employees. Capitalism has a face in the manager. (You may dislike that face but at least there is one.) Oversight responsibilities have been delegated to supervision bodies. Their task is to ensure that safety and labour laws are respected. In advanced economies, these institutions do their job. Now that retirement schemes have replaced home care for parents, no one wants to go back. Your brother-in-law is likely more fearful of the Food Safety and Inspection Services than he is of you. And chances are that his employees are no better off than those in large multinationals.

The drive for profit is not all bad news. Arguably, it means more resources allocated to the right places; the kind of places that develop a country and leverage on its people's creativity. It sounds like theoretical verbiage but this process does improve lives! By being less wasteful and hungry for opportunities, businesses play a key part in lifting the general wellbeing. Efficiency and creativity are necessary in order to maintain profitability. So it doesn't matter that the initial drive isn't that altruistic. After all, companies are still run by people. And (most) people have a sense of ethics.

Advanced economies need deep financial markets to improve the allocation of capital in their increasingly complex and decentralized system. Once infrastructures and basic services exist, it is not that easy to decide where money should go. Why do you think emerging nations try hard to foster a financial sector after the first stages of their development? The debate is beyond the scope of this book. Let's simply acknowledge that countries considered decent places to live in have found a controlled form of financial capitalism valuable.

Unlike your brother-in-law, listed firms make their *equity* accessible. Highly so. Anyone can acquire a piece of these businesses. The small and distant *retail investor* is protected by a series of laws and bodies. Their quality differs from one country to the next, depending on the legal system and history. But surprisingly (like so many things in our modern world), it works. It is more practical and affordable than ever to take part in the astonishing energy and creativity inside companies.

Why stock markets go up

We argue that businesses are the only thing worth owning. No asset class has beaten the broad stock market over the long run. Some listed companies disappear—others flourish. But overall, owning them, reinvesting the dividends and holding the position over long periods has delivered returns significantly higher than alternative forms of investments. Sovereign debt (issued by countries), corporate bonds, student loans or real estate do not match the long-term prospect of company stocks. One reason for this is risk. Shareholders take the sunshine as well as the heat. They receive whatever is left after all liabilities have been honoured. Reimbursing bondholders is one of them. Higher on the list is paying salaries and outstanding bills. In the financial world, more risk means more potential return. If a risky asset yields the same return as a safe one, investors turn to the latter. In turn, this lowers the relative price of the risky asset until it reflects its higher potential returns. This process establishes a "market price for risk". So much for self-pleasing academic theory. It never holds for too long but constitutes a good starting point.

The reason why stocks deliver higher returns is quite straightforward. Because it is trivial, we tend to neglect it. Consider for a moment what a business is: people getting out of bed (too) early, commuting to work (for too long) and devoting their energy to the production of ideas, goods and services. Sure, we all have indolent moments. Humans are not machines. Letting our minds wander is part of the process. But the point is that running an enterprise is a highly effective use of resources. How could idle capital do better? Let's compare a flat you own and rent out to a real estate company that does it as a business. No matter how ingenious and patient you are, you will never be as efficient. Likewise, you won't make bread as efficiently as your local baker.

Firms have access to economies of scale and strive towards best practices. They spend time focusing on this when you simply have better things to do. The real estate company will optimize its maintenance and accounting methods. It will rationalize its search for new tenants. It will employ loyal plumbers, electricians, construction workers and legal experts. Its bargaining power looms larger. We have all been exposed to the inefficiencies of organisations (in particular when we work for them). More can always be achieved. But overall, the soulless open space and depressing office is still where the magic happens! For all their lack of glamour, companies—large and small—are the devices that turn ideas into reality. They turn society's creativity and energy into wellbeing. Sometimes painfully, but they do.

Another source of superior return from stocks is the mistrust they generate. Most people do prefer brick and mortar. It is a general rule that thinking differently from the crowd is beneficial, as long as it is relevant. Steve Levitt, co-author of Freakonomics, has a very good way of putting it. Here is the advice he gives to students: "If you'd equally enjoy being a rock star and a chemist, go for chemistry." Common sense, you may say. But how often do you hear hesitant youngsters receive this piece of advice? They are often told to go for "the thing they like most". "Things will work out in the end if you put your mind to it." It's all very well intentioned. But there is cost and risk attached to sharing the same preferences as most! For example, people with unusual tastes regarding the opposite sex enjoy less competition. (Say, a man who prefers curvy women to the supermodel types.) In the realm of investment, the broad appeal of property explains its inferior yield.

The hot social debate around dividends deserves a word. Politicians dislike the fact that some companies would rather pay dividends than reinvest their profits. It is understandable since lower investment is a sign of faltering economic prospects. But the perception that paying dividends is a waste of resources is misguided. It is nothing more than businesses saying: "We don't know how to use this money". And in a way, this is healthy. Dividends are taxed and subsequently reallocated to alternative projects. They ensure that capital goes to productive uses instead of feeding the megalomaniac ambitions of already massive corporations. It would be great if more politicians knew when to pay dividends instead of perceiving extra revenue as a blank check for poorly assessed projects. The debate around the "1%" and the challenge to meritocracy is the relevant one. The focus on dividends is misguided.

All you need to know

"Democracy is the worst form of government, except all others", as Winston Churchill famously said. The same goes with investment. Low return, high risk, long commitment.... we are surrounded with options that are all bad. But we are surrounded by options nevertheless! Like the (relatively) clean air we breathe, we tend to take this for granted. In China and many emerging countries, *financial repression* is what prevails. Some feared its return in the aftermath of the 2008 recession. Financial repression refers to policies that constrain savers with the aim of exerting a "stealth tax" on returns. *Capital control* is one example. The maintenance of captive domestic markets for government debt is another. Mild forms of financial repression exist everywhere. They take the form of incentives to channel capital to certain uses (usually with good intentions).

No investment option is perfect. But some are better than others. There are many valid reasons for favouring brick and mortar. The point is not to turn you into an aggressive shareholder. Stock markets aren't for everyone. But they ought to be for far more people than currently is the case. At the very least, they deserve to appear on the list of boring options. The aim of this chapter is to demystify some of the concepts behind stock investing. We tend to look at prices as if they were pollen particles floating into a liquid. It doesn't help that many professionals do just that! *Brownian motions* and other concepts stem from the paradigm of physics. They offer a valuable framework to quantify things rigorously. But technicalities blind us from the original nature of financial assets.

High Expectations

Unlike natural sciences, economics is quite incapable of coming up with metrics that are consistent over time. The statement that "your current living standard is twenty times higher than that of your great-great-great-great grandfather" is highly questionable. What does "twenty times the conditions of a rural worker from the 19th century" even mean? How can we quantify the value of flying to the next country against walking to the next village? After all, the latter was as exotic at the time. How do we compare paid holidays with virtually no time for rest? Studies on happiness show that these concepts don't survive the scientific test. Your ancestor lived his life, with its tragedies and satisfactions. You live your own. Scales that work over a year make no sense over a century. The same goes with the statement that "wealth invested in stocks 120 years ago is now worth 1,000 times more in inflation-adjusted terms". The only interesting aspect is what it tells about the typical year: a long-term average return of 6%.

Another problem is what is called *survival bias*. Countries where abundant data is available (like the United States) are likely to be precisely those that succeeded. They survived by definition! No one comes up with figures on what it would have been like to invest in Mesopotamia over the last two millennia, or in the Ottoman Empire over the previous century. You need stability to produce the data, and stability itself introduces a bias. In *Rational Expectations*, William J. Bernstein mentions another interesting limitation. Discussing the high average stock return measured in the U.S. over the long run, he points out that the very access to stock markets was much more limited than it is today. Transaction costs were enormous. The informational and social edge needed to even consider entering these trades make these high returns misleading. A more reasonable assertion is that equities have shown to be the most rewarding asset class in developed economies over time.

First-mover advantage refers to the gain captured by the initial occupant of a market segment. The monopoly-like status enjoyed is supposedly short-lived as new entrants compete more effectively. The housing market and higher education are good examples. As more people understand their value, they have become less of a bargain. Post-war real-estate performance boomed as access to credit developed. This form of democratization should be celebrated, even if it led to the abuses of subprime mortgages. Asset prices merely catch up with the value that their expected cash flow justifies. After housing, education has been the next inefficiency tackled by financial reasoning. *The Economist* reported in June 2014 that student loan debt exceeded U.S.$1.2 trillion. Education services are becoming more expensive as more people understand their value. This is nothing but the result of the greater number making better decisions. In the past, education wasn't more accessible despite its lower price. A smaller share of the population achieved it, which is the bottom line! The price of something is only one dimension of its accessibility. Information is another. Let's face it; rich kids simply go to college because they are told to do so.

Our objective is to expand awareness in the realm of investment, even if this means dissolving the first-mover advantage. If the majority were to make smart decisions, these decisions wouldn't be very smart anymore. The good news is that new prospects come up just as fast as old ones disappear. Finance is about disconnecting the source of capital from its use. Note that you most likely wouldn't invest in our brother-in-law's restaurant. But you happily let complete strangers manage your assets! This takes both information and trust. You understand that it is unlikely for your brother-in-law to offer the best deal in town. And you trust the institutions that protect your money beyond the immediate circle. The process called *financial deepening* refers to the increased provision of financial services in society as a whole. In primitive economies, loans would only be made within a narrow circle of trust, which was a waste on creativity and imagination.

We explained that investment is not a zero-sum game. But the size of the pie is limited nevertheless. What is it bounded by? Let's bear in mind some aggregates. Like gravity, they bring us back to Earth when we need to. The growth rate of world GDP is one of them. Remember that the United

States has become the United States (i.e. the largest economy in the history of mankind) by growing at a mere 2% over a couple of centuries. If anything, this figure illustrates the power of *compounding*. I personally discovered it early in life, via household debt rather than investments. Seemingly manageable interest rates turn into bottomless pits of debt. My parents, low earners but arguably educated people (one of them a math teacher!), were fooled by the power of compounding. Something that grows 7% a year will take no more than a decade to double up. After three decades, it will be eight times as large. This is how China has grown into becoming—adjusted for purchasing power—the largest economy on the planet in 2014.

According to the International Monetary Fund, world growth in real terms has averaged 3.8% over the past 50 years. From a historical perspective, this figure is remarkable. It is a cause for optimism, as long as it can happen in harmony with the environment. Ending possession is one way to get there! It shows the exceptional dynamism of our times (if you ever doubted it). This number should be to finance what the speed of light is to physics: an upper bound. If total capital yield outpaces this rate, it means that the share of production devoted to paying capital (as opposed to labour) grows. Such state of affairs is unsustainable in the long run. Even the most docile workers (including yourself and this author) would not tolerate it. Thomas Piketty's *Capital in the 21st Century* is a reminder of the importance of underlying "laws of gravity". The total stock of capital and its growth rate cannot sustainably diverge from the production of wealth in the economy.

Putting a number on future returns from stock markets is hazardous. But because safer assets typically yield less than world growth, high expectation is justified. Will economic expansion come to a halt due to the exhaustion of resources and opportunities? (The so-called *secular stagnation*.) Will it remain similar to the past century? Will technology and artificial intelligence disrupt the model entirely? The *technological singularity* theory suggests that the invention of a self-improving machine would put an end to progress, as we know it. An *intelligence explosion* would make the process so fast that it would surpass our ability to understand or control it. No scenario can be dismissed. We shall simply stick to the fact that, in the foreseeable future, enterprises are still the place where growth and innovation happens.

Diversification

A powerful drag toward homeownership is the notion that "no matter how wrong things go, you can always live in a home". In other words, its value cannot fall to zero. It is not the case for a company. Companies go bankrupt every day. This observation is correct. Unfortunately, it keeps reasonable investors at bay when they should not. As always, providing the right answer to the wrong question doesn't help. The right question to ask is the following: can we benefit from the high returns of businesses without suffering from their intrinsically fragile nature? The answer to this question is yes. *Diversification* is the most basic concept in investment. It simply means that one should not put all his or her eggs in one basket. And yet most retail investors choose to plainly ignore it.

Market experts know the great hazard of picking stocks. Meanwhile, "good family men" take exorbitant risks, without even realizing it. They do it partly because of the myths exposed in Part 1. People assume that the whole point about stocks is making bets! This is madness or plain gambling. Another typical example is Equity Incentive Plans. Making employees invest in the shares of their own company is one of the most terrible ideas that financial capitalism has ever come up with (and it came up with a few). Not only do you end up putting too many eggs in one basket, you also link your investment's performance to your job situation. If the company flourishes, it is a bonanza. If it struggles, you lose on all fronts. Not to mention that in the typically large companies that implement such plans, the connection between individual performance and stock price is dubious. No matter how hard a single employee works, he or she won't have much impact on the stock price. Even CEOs may not matter much! The topic is controversial in academic literature but recent studies find a "CEO effect" on profit ranging from 4% to 13%. Diversification is the acceptance of our own ignorance.

Tim Wardle, a British documentary maker, travelled the U.K. for a production called *In Search of Mr Average*. After a long quest, he identified a man whose income, age, weight, lifestyle, tastes, number of children, etc. best fit the average British person. One individual can display characteristics that are similar to the group as a whole. Obviously, the exercise does not work for all dimensions. Only some, like longevity or income can be averaged. The gender of a person is specific while the average is half woman-half man. Likewise, the average person would be Christian, Muslim, Jewish, Atheist and Agnostic all at the same time!

Things are similar with companies. The return to expect from a given firm in a given sector can be drawn from the group. So can the likeliness of bankruptcy over the next decade. But a large group of companies does not behave like a single business when it comes to extinction. Just like the average British person does not die, the average firm does not see its value fall to zero. That is to say that possessing a small piece from hundreds of businesses does not produce the intrinsic fragility of the single firm. A diversified portfolio is more than mere risk mitigation. It changes the very nature of stock investment. The market as a whole is under no threat to become worthless. Of course, it means that some of the desirable features of companies are also lost. The average company is pretty boring! The success stories you see in individual firms don't exist here. (When they do, they are a strong signal for a bubble in the making.)

Businesses are the best at turning one dollar into something more. But a full range of options exists. Sovereign debt (lending money to a state) is an alternative for those who cannot cope with the risks involved by stock holdings. Every time someone ticks the "conservative" option on a retirement plan, they are buying more of the treasuries issued by their country. Corporate debt is another option that lies in-between in terms of risk. Company creditors have priority over equity holders in case of financial hardship and they typically ask for higher returns than sovereign debt. The point is that you don't need to understand everything about these technicalities. Each type simply involves a different risk-return profile.

Diversification keeps room for brick and mortar. After all, it is one of the many productive uses of capital. There is just no reason to consider it naturally superior. If it were, institutional investors of the world would pour all of their resources into real estate. As a matter of fact, they do not. Portfolio managers (whose role is to decide on the asset allocation of pension funds and other investment mammoths) diversify into a variety of assets in order to optimize their risk-return profile. So should you.

Volatility (and why we abhor it)

Daniel Kahneman is a psychologist who specializes in judgment and decision-making. He was awarded the Nobel Memorial Prize in Economics in 2002 for his work on behavioural finance. His book, *Thinking, Fast and Slow* is an enjoyable read for anyone who has interest in the intricacies of the human brain. In one interview with the German magazine *Der Spiegel*, he discusses the way our memory works with the following example:

"Someone once told me that he had recently listened to a wonderful symphony but, unfortunately, at the end, there was a terrible screeching sound on the record. He said that ruined the whole experience. But, of course, the only thing it ruined was the memory of the experience, (which was) still a happy experience."

Our past experiences make us who we are. They allow us to make better decisions in the future. But they only exist in the form of memories. And memories are prone to biases for merely technical reasons. We are lazy (another way to say "efficient"). We recognize that remembering the full details of events with equal weight is tedious and unnecessary. Better limit storage to the most striking features and the lesson learned. The *rest of it*—even if it happens to be *most of it*—can be remembered as a vague impression that receives less importance. As Kahneman notes, *"From the evolutionary point of view, that makes sense. The duration of an experience is simply not relevant. What matters for survival is whether it ended well and how bad it got. This also applies to animals."*

It offers a glimpse into why our intuition is so bad at assessing risk. We are born storytellers. The tendency to focus on narratives has been serving us well. It allows anticipating (if not predicting) the future course of events, and promotes our imagination. But it has made us bad at assessing the relative weight of different risks. For example, we know that flying is safe. Yet we cannot help feeling a slight shudder as we leave the tarmac wrapped up in tons of metal. Meanwhile, stepping inside a coach feels rather benign. Parents worry about sexual psychopaths and sadly underestimate the risks associated with private swimming pools.

Likewise, market crashes and headline bankruptcies attract most of the attention. We tend to judge the risk posed by stock markets from the most frightening story we have heard of. *"Markets are down 5%"*; *"Volkswagen just erased a third of its value."* These experiences are frequently thrown in the face of the equity investor. No such thing with treasury bills or homes. The true story told by stock markets (that no one can hear because it is whispered) is that indexes increase 0.02% a day on average. A tiny increase that doubles their value over a decade! As commentators like to say, markets take the stairs up and the elevator down. Professionals are even more prone to short-sightedness because their memory is full of "war stories". What captures their attention is "how bad it got". In behavioural finance, this is referred to as *regrets*. Instead of maximizing what we might gain, we often prefer minimizing what we might lose.

As a result, people pay an eccentric price for safety. Our biases make risk-taking highly profitable. This is good news for those willing to take it. Again, thinking differently from the crowd is beneficial. The gap between the yield of the safest financial assets and that of risky ones is close to 4 percentage points. Given the power of compounding, this is gigantic. The former type (typically U.S. Treasury Bills) yields an annual return close to 2% over long periods. The latter (typically equities) delivers 6%. Obviously, volatility is higher. But diversification makes volatility manageable.

We are talking about owning a tiny piece of all the types of businesses that exist (as long as they are large enough to be listed on an exchange). This means restaurant chains, technology companies, car manufacturers, utilities, energy, entertainment... even real estate! It means being exposed to many countries. If one encounters difficulties due to specific circumstances, another might fetch better. Again, the whole is different in nature from its parts. I insist. Financial assets are perceived as fragile because they represent no more than zeros and ones on a hard disk. But the risk for a well-diversified portfolio to become worthless is global-nuclear-war minuscule. The conventional assumption that brick and mortar is better sheltered against such *tail risk* is misguided. A revolution that, say, puts an end to the very institution of private property would hit real estate as much as financial assets. (It need not be a bad thing as long as we invent something better.) Maybe the disruption will come from automation being so advanced that art becomes the only form of value! Who knows? Whatever happens, encompassing a large variety of activities is more robust than sticking to four walls and a roof.

Over a given year, diversified indexes like the S&P500 typically move up or down within a range of +/-15%. The worst yearly drop since 1950 happened in 2008 when it lost 38%. This magnitude is no larger than busting housing bubbles. Another important metric is what is called the *drawdown*. It refers to the largest percentage loss from market peak to bottom. By definition, drawdowns can be severe. The last financial crisis caused a 53% decrease from October 2007 to March 2009. Prior to that, the worse was 46% (from October 2000 to September 2002). Don't let these numbers frighten you. One rarely enters the market at the top to exit at the bottom. But they are interesting because they show that value can easily halve. Drawdowns wipe out leveraged investors like wild horses in a rodeo.

At this point, it is worth discussing the limitation of existing measures. If approached wisely, financial markets are not as perilous as most people assume. But this should not lead to overconfidence. The concept of "volatility" is overused as much as it is obscure. It has a clear mathematical formulation as the standard deviation of return over a given time horizon. But the jargon should fool no one. As a social construction, asset prices do not follow any predetermined law. Adding complexity to the maths does not change this fact. This is where *hard science* collides with *social science*. The inability to be exact does not make measurement useless. Orders of magnitude mean something as long as the limitations are understood. Nassim Nicholas Taleb's insightful *Black Swan* is a compulsory read for anyone who wants to be serious about risk. The author asserts that the unexpected is what eventually drives the world. Averages and bell curves (that describe what happens under "normal circumstances") are useful most of the time, expect when it really matters.

I personally admire Taleb and generally agree with the case he raises. He reminds us that, like Frankenstein, statistical concepts run out of control. They do so when we fool ourselves about their scientific significance. But empiricism is treacherous in its own ways. By definition, data is neutral (though the way it is presented never is). Data contains no view regarding what might be because it is only about what has been. It is uninterested in the *why* and focuses on the *what*. Big Data allows machines to "act smart" by crunching enormous amounts of information. Unlike theory, empiricism is unable to foresee the unseen or explain why we observe what we observe. Our strong focus on *qualitative* analysis—as opposed to a *quantitative* one—is deliberate. Historical volatility and past returns are useful to figure out what to expect. But the main argument we make in favour of equity is a theoretical one: running a business is an efficient use of resources. It is therefore natural that it should offer good prospects.

Critics challenged Taleb over his lack of proposition for an alternative approach. His message was seen as unconstructive. There is only so much one can cover in a single book. The object of the *Black Swan* was not to propose solutions. They would come in Taleb's following opus, *Antifragile*. The central proposition of this work is that risk cannot be assessed well. So forget about predicting the future! The best way to protect ourselves is to nurture a desirable property he calls *Antifragility*. In its most simple form, *Antifragility* is the capacity for a system to reinforce itself in the event of a shock. This is very different from the ability to resist shocks. (Which would be a form of *robustness*.) It all seems rather abstract but there are examples of such systems.

If the Constitution of the United States has been able to survive longer than most of its European counterparts, it is mostly because it was designed in a way that it could absorb the unpredictable contradictions that society would exert on it. America's Founding Fathers were careful enough to stick to general principles without yielding to the temptation of making assumptions about the world to come. In other words, they embraced unpredictability. This was unlike the Treaty establishing a Constitution for Europe. Rejected by voters in 2005, it contained stores of details (including the nature of the production system as a market economy). A system that learns from its shocks, no matter how wobbly, is preferable to one that offers the appearance of stability. The U.S. Congress looks on the brink of collapse every year, when it stalls due to fierce partisan debates. But it is the rigid regimes of the Middle East that collapsed under the assault of the Arab Spring. Bamboo is stronger than steel. The volatility of financial assets reflects their capacity to absorb shocks. On the other hand, the reassuring immobility of real estate conceals its inherent fragility.

The discrete virtues of patience

We exposed why a diversified portfolio mitigates the ups and downs that individual companies naturally encounter. If company A is doing poorly due to a strategy that turned sour, company B may bounce back. When the technology sector disappoints because demand for gadgets is saturated, car manufacturers may boom due to an unexpectedly strong demand. By including hundreds of companies from possibly dozens of countries, large portfolios obtain a behaviour that is closer to "the typical company under normal circumstances" (this imaginary object that does not go bankrupt and delivers decent returns). In this case, picking the *wrong company* is the risk we try to alleviate. Let's call this *horizontal* diversification. Another potential pitfall is buying at the *wrong time*. If one holds a group of businesses for a single year, the chances to end up with a very good or very bad outcome are high. But over decades, good times will compensate turbulent ones. The natural channel to mitigate this risk is to give the exposure more time. Let's call this *vertical* diversification. A classic joke is that a long-term investment is nothing more than a short-term one that turned bad. And it sometimes is. But the key message is that time is on your side.

Why do such "bad years" even exist on the market as a whole? After all, companies go their separate ways. They deal with different markets and constraints, across different industries and continents. The answer is another jargon term (even more obscure than *volatility*) called *correlation*. It describes the way separate variables may evolve in lockstep over a given timeframe. We all intuitively understand that there is such a thing as a state of the global economy. During the Great Recession, most companies suffered, even if some flourished. Correlation is a simple statistical measure of "how synchronized" these cycles are. Unsurprisingly, two American car manufactures are more correlated than a Chinese bank and an Italian law firm. (Unlike bankers, lawyers seem to benefit from the good times as much as the bad ones.) The point is that high correlation is bad because it hinders risk mitigation. If all firms were evolving in perfect lockstep (a correlation of 1), there would be no point at all in *horizontal* diversification. The good news is that they do not.

Correlation is sensitive to time horizon. This brings us back to another virtue of patience that is underappreciated. As time horizon increases, this apparent synchronization between apparently similar entities wears out. This is a point that even finance professionals fail to appreciate because their day-to-day time horizon is short. They talk about "correlation" as if it had no time dependence when it clearly does. We should only talk about "correlation over a given horizon".

Over a single day, correlation is strong. This is because the specific conditions of a given company do not change so rapidly. No matter how many analysts scrutinize the slightest change in the CEO's haircut, meaningful information about a company does not come up daily! In its absence, changes in the external environment become the main driver of price moves. If there is nothing different from yesterday to judge the financial health of company X, the general state of the economy is the news. Maybe the Fed announced a rate cut or business sentiment is down. Our Chinese bank and Italian law firm are likely to appear surprisingly connected. Over the long run, the picture is totally different. Correlation is very weak. The fortunes of two firms will diverge entirely over decades or a generation! Small differences accumulate until one of them becomes the undisputed leader while its competitors are struggling to defend a meagre market share.

How effective is vertical diversification? Data is based on what has been. And as we explained, the past should be treated with care. But the point is to appreciate the magnitude of the effect. Picking any given year from 1926 onward to invest in the main American index had a 27% chance to be a losing bet. The same exercise over a given 10-year period brings it down to 5%. Over 30 years, the chance of losing money is minuscule. The cause for this lies in the conjunction of two effects. As the time horizon doubles, risk increases. But it does not double. We say that it is "non-linear". Risk increases more and more slowly (a property called "concavity"). Meanwhile, the expected return is the opposite! It does more than double under the effect of compounding. (We say that it is "convex".) The result is that risk and return go their separate ways. The former becomes ever smaller relative to the latter.

Equities only represent a gamble when approached in a rogue manner. With caution and patience, stock markets are nowhere as hazardous as we intuitively assume. Unfortunately, studies show that the typical period for which retail investors hold an exposure to stocks is only 3 years. In addition to the risk it induces, market timing is usually pretty bad. Small savers tend to sell before the market bounces back and buy before it falls. People aren't as impatient with alternative assets like real estate, which are held for decades. The perception that financial markets are playgrounds for gamblers is somehow self-fulfilling. As long as it prevails, reasonable people will keep their personal savings out of it.

Anchoring and other oddities

On a trip to Argentina, I found myself running out of U.S. dollars. It proved a perfect experiment for two well-documented effects: *anchoring* and *relativity of prices*. After a long history of financial instability, the country opted for capital controls. An official rate officially allowed Argentineans to buy dollars "cheaply" (8 pesos for 1 dollar at the time). In fact, these dollars were heavily rationed. A black market emerged as a result. U.S. dollars could be exchanged on the street for as high as 13 pesos. (This regime was ended in 2015 after the election of Mauricio Macri.) People called it the *blue rate* and all tourists visiting Argentina knew about it. They would bring dollars in cash in order to avoid the phony official rate. By the end of the stay, I was running out of dollars. (The reason why we always underestimate future spending is another bias worth investigating. Maybe we are natural-born optimists?) The result simply meant that I had to withdraw cash at the disadvantageous official rate... Suddenly, all the prices I was facing were 63%

higher than what I was used to. Worse, I knew that it was not the case for fellow travellers with better planning skills than mine. Finally, I couldn't help but cut on my consumptions and finish the trip on a shoestring.

By any measure, prices at the official rate were still reasonable. I was spending less on each cup of coffee than I would have at home! But at home, the playing field was even. My treatment was the same as the next guy and no different from the previous day. Paying a much higher price than my previous habit (the *anchor*) and the person next to me (the *relativity* effect) felt outrageous. Dan Ariely exposes these effects in *Predictably Irrational*. Being sensitive to relative prices is rational. What's not is the way we integrate this totally arbitrary reference. When humans have no idea what something is worth, the first price they see is the financial equivalent of their mother's voice. It is a benchmark they take for granted and measure everything else against. This is why asset bubbles can inflate to levels that seem outlandish after the burst.

Another key concept is the notion of *opportunity cost*. Life is filled with two distinct types of mistakes. The things we regret having done, and the things we regret not having done. For some reason, our brains are much more sensitive to the first type. An investor who's made a wrong decision by, say, betting on Nokia will feel more regrets than one who failed to bet on Apple. The loss made on the Nokia investment is what economists call *sunk cost*. The other type, caused by not betting on Apple, is an *opportunity cost.*

We are very familiar with sunk costs. The jobs we quit and the relationships we end are sunk costs. Something we had and no longer possess. But those same jobs and relationships were also preventing us from pursuing different lives—like a parallel universe in which we might be happier. In this sense, they entail an opportunity cost. Granted, too much of such thinking seems like a direct road to a life of disappointment and frustration. But a little of it is useful. It reminds us that risk goes both ways.

The gains we occasionally miss by failing to be exposed (opportunity cost) are not intrinsically different from the losses we make from being exposed (sunk cost). From this perspective, having no exposure is somehow as "risky" as having some! It seems far-fetched. But just ask Mark Zuckerberg's former college roommate. Based on his father's advice, he turned down an invitation to help start Facebook in order to complete graduation.

Market efficiency

On a flight from La Paz to the Bolivian city of Uyuni, I found myself sitting next to the country head of a large Swiss asset manager. It was shortly after the election of Alexis Tsipras as the new Prime Minister of Greece. On your way to the Bolivian desert, a compatriot is a reassuring thing. The French man was open and friendly. Realizing that I was also in banking, he couldn't help discuss recent market trends. His wife rolled her eyes, as the topic filled him with excitement. He was pessimistic about Greece and had made large bets accordingly. But the man was frustrated. The far left's victory had been a landslide. An extremist party was now heading a member state of the respectable euro zone! Syriza was about to overrule all previous agreements. In other words, he had made the right call. The world was about to end and he had bet in this direction. And yet, he was losing money. European markets were up when they reopened that Monday!

If this was puzzling for an experienced professional like him, it must be for most mortals. However, it was nothing more than another day on financial markets. First of all, such bets are not investment. They are plain gambling. Some derive pleasure from them; so be it. But don't fool yourself into thinking that "the elite knows better". Witness the surprise caused by the outcome of the United Kingdom EU membership referendum (leading to the so-called "Brexit"). Another reminder is the desperation with which Chinese leaders tried in vain to limit the stock market crash of 2015. When it comes to predicting or controlling prices, even the top of the food chain is helpless. This is good news and let's explain why.

The bus allegory

Imagine that an odd task has been assigned to you: estimating the remaining duration of your lifetime. You must do so as precisely as possible, constantly readjusting the prediction. Like the rest of us, you (fortunately) do not know the answer. But you have some information. For example, an extra century is probably out of the question. Age, gender, occupation and so on, can help you refine your estimate. New information will also lead to revisions. For example, you might witness a growing pollution problem in your city (say, if you live in Beijing). You initially incorporated a rate of life expectancy increase similar to what your parents enjoyed. You did not expect pollution to grow so serious, and gradually acknowledge that the healthier aspects of your lifestyle will be somewhat "compensated" by the bad air you breathe. You adjust your initial prediction down slightly. Of course, surprises can also be on the upside. For example, if a miraculous new drug is invented.

Assume that you are taking this task seriously. You are keeping track of your estimate. It is drawn on a chart with its ups and downs, and updated continuously till the end of your life. (The health-tracking gadget fad is making this terrifying prospect plausible!) The chart is smooth overall, with a gentle downward trend as time goes by. It features steeper changes corresponding to the rare occasions when you received new and relevant information impacting your evaluation. A serious escalation between your country and a superpower caused a sharp fall. It gradually climbed back up as the tensions eased. You had promised to quit but are craving a smoke. You decide to leave your building and buy cigarettes. The curve decreases imperceptibly. While crossing the street, a scene catches your attention. Focusing back on your track, you notice a bus coming straight at you. The distance is too short and it is coming too fast. The curve drops from 50 years to 1 second.

This thought experiment illustrates the process that drives asset prices. Simply replace the remaining lifetime with the remaining cash flow. What series of rents can one expect from this house? What will the profits of this young company look like in the future? The price movement of an asset is not about its *past* merits. Ups and downs are all about new information and how it impacts the *future*. If a large company is showing interest in a start-up, it will cause its price to surge. The rumour itself will also have an impact because the mere likeliness of the deal is relevant. New information alters the prediction and reflects it in the price. Price moves can stem from any form of intelligence as long as it is *new*. It can be something exogenous (a world crisis) or endogenous (bad management). The point is that price moves are all about the future. And predicting the future is a difficult business! Weather forecasters, political experts, and economists make predictions at short time horizons and fail. It is therefore no surprise that the price-formation process is so erratic.

How well and how fast is new intelligence absorbed by prices determines the degree of *market efficiency*. In other words, it is the price's ability to digest information. This concept is probably one of the most misinterpreted. Arguing that markets are "efficient" does not entail that prices are accurate and bubbles won't form. Averting volatility would require being able to predict the future. And no one or nothing is good at predicting the future. Some are simply worse than others.

Evidence

Are financial markets really efficient? The question is open but some things can be said. The first theoretical consequence of market efficiency is unpredictability. If the current price already reflects all available knowledge, there is no point in trying to infer the future price from any existing piece of information. In particular, the path that led to the current level should be valueless (a so-called *Markov property*). Think about the last time you saw a price chart. If you are a member of the human species, your brain was inferring the future without even asking for permission. This is foolish! Broad statistical evidence suggests that the price path is typically useless for making predictions. This very fact establishes the existence of a mild form of efficiency.

What about bubbles? Don't they prove that markets are irrational? Isn't volatility a sign that markets aren't doing their job? Deconstructing this chain of thought is where the *bus allegory* helps. The mere existence of steep readjustment is no obvious sign of irrationality or inability to process information. It can be. But it merely reflects the complexity of the world. Its chaotic nature is prone to *butterfly effects*. You had no way to foresee the bus incident before it was too late. A tiny nudge in initial conditions translates into dramatically different outcomes. (It was "so close to never happening".) In other words, stock prices are volatile primarily because the future is volatile. And the news that markets cannot predict the future—the only way to get rid of volatility—is really no news at all!

Another misconception is that counterintuitive market moves (prices dropping on a good news, surging on a bad one) are an expression of irrationality. Again, remember that predictability would actually defeat efficiency! Before any official announcement is done (macroeconomic figures, company results, key interest rates) markets formulate an opinion. Their job is to predict, not to acknowledge the initial intention. If these predictions aren't biased (*i.e.* they overestimate as often as they underestimate), it is only natural that positive announcements can trigger price falls as much as surges. The moment a piece of information becomes reliable is not clear-cut; hence the key role of early indicators. "Buy the rumour, sell the news" as the old adage goes. Don't waste your energy. Unless you are in a specific position with superior knowledge or resources, you will always know "too late". (And if you have insider information, trading on it is illegal anyway.)

Obviously, evidence is mixed and denying some irrationality would be pure ideology. *Behavioural finance* is full of fascinating examples. Unlike the bus allegory, not all market bubbles can be justified by an element of surprise in relevant information. Some form of exuberance is always at play. Investors are subject to *herd behaviour*. Instead of taking a step back and assessing the situation, they mimic each other in what becomes a self-enforcing process.

A remarkable feature of bubble formation is the acceptance we have for the post-bubble story. The very fact that prices collapsed is enough for us to accept the new (low) valuation as the correct one. We are caught taking the current price for granted once again; exactly what causes bubbles to inflate in the first place! In reality, there is no more reason to trust it than the previous "exuberant" level. After the 2000 Dot-com crisis, the story was that people had been mad to believe that companies making no revenue could be worth billions of dollars. But aren't bubble busts as irrational as bubbles themselves? As Daniel Kahneman notes, we are much more receptive to good stories than to the kind of evidence that cold-blooded statistics produces.

Let's concede that people generally don't do crazy things with their money. Being wrong is not the same as being irrational. This author's view is that scholars are often too prompt at ruling out the *efficiency hypothesis*. Just like economists are too prompt at dismissing the *homo economicus* (the hypothesis that agents make rational decisions). It sounds smarter to say that "things are more complicated" because they always are. But this is how one ends up saying nothing at all. Concepts should be taken for what they are: a tool to comprehend reality. The absence of perfect circles in nature does not make the concept of a circle irrelevant. So let's play devil's advocate. It's so much more fun.

Faster than its shadow

Markets are not only fast at digesting *public* information. They are often the first place where *private* information is made publicly available. It means that prices become the source of information itself. The reason is simple. People with enough certitude about a fact to put *skin in the game* will benefit from revealing it through trading. Whether this confidence stems from an advanced way to process data (pattern recognition, talented market analysts) or criminal insider information is of little importance to you (though it is in the eyes of the law). It needs only be statistically correct as opposed to absolutely certain. The point is that better-informed participants have a strong incentive to distribute information through buying and selling rather than calling the media. This is why a nation-wide survey on estimating the fair price for oil will be less informative than what open markets make publicly available.

This means that current prices are *de facto* information. It is a fast form of information that brutally simplifies reality. It lives in one single dimension: up or down. Think of it as hearing someone shout, "watch out!" before even understanding what is going on. You would certainly consider this warning and take action. But at this stage, you have no clue if running or protecting your head is the best call. Now, try to picture... an economy. If you think you succeeded, think again. Economies are complex beasts, extremely so. Their intricacies cannot be captured in a single thought, and certainly not real-time. Economists need months and years to reconcile a vague picture of the situation. "Picture" is the appropriate term because experts must project a complex reality into fewer dimensions (GDP, unemployment, business sentiment...). These snapshots have colours and help assess the situation. But it takes months to develop them! Market prices, on the other hand, are fast at capturing the current state of the economy. But they are an even simpler projection, like a shadow.

Events like the *2010 Flash Crash* are an illustration. On May 6th, the Dow Jones plunged 9% within minutes, recovering shortly after. The initial price fall that caused the chain reaction appeared trivial after the fact. But at the time, it was new information that something big was happening. Over short timeframes, markets feed on the intelligence they produce faster than the time it takes to recoup the evidence. It is as if this extraordinary information-absorption machine was digesting itself! Being afraid of your own shadow does not lead to very smart decisions. Ironically, it is the high degree of market efficiency that undermines efficiency itself.

As Michael Lewis' *Flash Boys* shows, the benign approach to trading speed from regulators proved misguided. Sophisticated participants are able to seek rents without adding value to the price-formation process. The average guy will always be too slow. This was already the case in the not-too-distant past when "fast" meant hours. It does not really matter how fast others are as long as they are faster than you. But let's illustrate how extreme things have become with a factual example.

It was 1:07pm on April 23rd, 2013. The Associated Press Twitter account sent the following message on its feed: "Breaking: Two Explosions in the White House and Barack Obama is injured." Nine minutes later, the Associated Press confirmed that its account had been hacked and the news was a fake. For the vast majority, the story went too fast to even start worrying. But on currency and equity markets, the hack caused a drop that wiped out $130 billion in value! Prices recovered quickly after the scam was revealed. What's interesting about this incident is not just the scale of the drop, which demonstrates how fragile liquidity can be when everyone rushes to the door. It highlights that not everyone rushes to the door at the same speed! We know that some participants are faster than others at digesting news.

But this event helped measure it precisely. It was the perfect *market efficiency* experiment.

The first aggressive sell order was sent out just a few seconds after the tweet publication. In the time it takes you to read this sentence, trading algorithms have been able to scan through thousands of news sent from various sources. Not only will they spot big announcements long before anyone else—these programs will act on them, as they did on April 23rd. Robots (still) cannot appreciate literature. But their ability to interpret language is advancing fast. Today's *artificial intelligence* is advanced enough to mimic the kind of animal reaction that a panicking human would take. Hedge funds and high-frequency firms are heavily investing in the field of *unstructured data* analysis. You may laugh at them for being fooled by the Twitter scam. But for this one occurrence, think about the number of official announcement and legitimate intelligence that was processed fast enough to yield a profit.

What looks like science fiction or paranoia is really not. The new frontier for advanced market signals is... outer space. Satellite images combined with big-data software are what former NASA scientist James Crawford calls "macroscopes". In real-time, they capture things that are too large for the human eye: light intensity at night, storage facilities, trucks in factories' parking lots. Interest in them comes from policy makers as much as Wall Street. Weeks before a survey-based GDP correction is completed, these images can anticipate the outcome. Planet Labs, BlackSky Global, Spaceknow, Orbital

Insight (and other evil-sounding companies) are investing billions in satellite fleets and processing capacity. You simply cannot win this race. But the good news is that it doesn't matter. Who wants to spend his days on Twitter anyway?

What it means for you

The American economist Eugene Fama is the father of the *efficient-market hypothesis*. He sums it up with these words: "I take the market efficiency hypothesis to be the simple statement that security prices fully reflect all available information." His paradigm has been challenged by alternative approaches that stress the irrationality of economic agents. This field, called *behavioural finance,* is both fun and relevant. But it does not abolish the principle that Fama framed. Instead, it enriches it enormously. Therefore, it is not surprising that he shared the 2013 Nobel Memorial Prize in Economics with Robert J. Shiller, who outlined the "irrational exuberance" of markets. These theories do not need to be mutually exclusive.

Free prices act like a continuous large-scale survey. When investing in something, one imperceptibly drives the whole economy in that direction. For example, you might allocate capital towards emerging countries by acquiring their sovereign bonds. For what the initial reason is worth, you put *skin in the game*. You will lose money if this view proves misguided. And people express different opinions when they have skin in the game. Everyone has a view on everything. But they won't put their shirt on it.

What's the point, then? Why throw your hard working money into this pool full of sharks? Well, simply because you don't have to fight them! Just let yourself drift with the current. Efficiency is good news because it ensures that prices keep track with reality, which is all you need. Even if it means that easy opportunities don't exist. ("There is no such thing as a free lunch.") You don't need to worry about taking views like favouring small companies or high-dividend ones. Any obvious premium or discount is already priced in. In other words, it is fine to be lazy. All you have to do is diversify and stay patient. You know nothing about the short term. You know nothing about the medium term. But you know everything about the long term. You may focus on enjoying your most valuable asset: time. Relax, read, watch movies and spend quality time with your loved ones instead of losing yourself in financial reports. Remember, this is no *zero sum game*. The pie grows. Erratically; but it grows.

Saving in the Digital Age

Discrete virtues

Risk and *return* are the features that first come to mind when considering an investment. In the classic framework, one's objective is to maximize return under a given risk. Yet there are far more dimensions worth considering. In the real world, they are precisely what make homeownership desirable for most. "Can I touch it?" "Does it act like a social signal?" "Is it marked-to-market?" "Will it be binding?" "Is it ethical?" There are valid reasons why other dimensions should eclipse the risk and return paradigm. People aren't senseless. But we want to approach them differently. Financial assets possess qualities that are vastly underappreciated. They have more to offer than "attractive returns under managed risk".

Urbanization was more than a way to increase the productivity of workers. It proposed a new *way of life*. Likewise, modern finance is more than the democratisation of access to business ownership. Embracing the possibilities of greater dependence on others is the history of economics (if not mankind). It means reassessing our animal instincts, even when they carry a fair share of wisdom. The (apparent) immaterial nature of financial assets is not a necessary evil but a desirable feature! It means more transparency and freedom.

A whole spectrum of financial assets exists, eventually relying on businesses. And there are simple ways to benefit from them. After exposing the big picture, it is time to explain how to practically embrace the *end of possession*. We aim to promote a boring model (passive diversification) on an exciting asset class (companies) rather than an exciting model (leverage) on a boring asset class (property).

Liquidity, mon amour

A key dimension besides risk and return is *liquidity*. An asset is deemed liquid if "it can be bought or sold rapidly without incurring a significant cost". Of course, the notion of rapidity is somewhat subjective. It refers to a relative degree between assets. Cash is perfectly liquid because I suffer no *discount* when transacting. In other words, spending hastily does not reduce the value of the notes in my pocket. The story is different if I must sell a car in a hurry in order to cover up some expense. I will have to discount it. Low liquidity makes haste expensive. Instead of advertising it at a decent price and waiting for a willing buyer, the person initiating the trade must adjust to what is currently available. In other words, when *shit hits the fan*, you want your assets to be liquid.

A friend of this author once found himself selling an automobile to a young couple. They liked the car. He liked them. Before closing the deal, he decided he would offer a discount. Instead of seeing it as a considerate gesture, their reaction was to cancel the transaction. His offer was interpreted as a signal that some hidden defect must exist. Surely, if the price was reduced for no obvious reason, the car must be faulty!

This story illustrates the concept of *information asymmetry*. Georges Akerlof received the Nobel Memorial Prize in Economics for a 1970 paper that examined precisely the market for second-hand cars. When sellers possess more information than buyers on the good being sold, a discount is priced-in. This discount accounts for the expected defects—even if the good is perfectly fine. The mere chance that there exists some defect reduces the price tag. It cannot be as high as a well-maintained equivalent for which no information asymmetry exists. Sellers of well-maintained cars are penalized by the rogue behaviour of their peers; like a good student from a bad school. If I were to tell you nothing about a man outside the fact that he is a banker, he would surely struggle to gain your esteem. (Even bankers mistrust bankers.) This penalty drives out of the market those for which it is most unfair: the virtuous sellers. Information asymmetry can also be on the buyer's side, for example in insurance contracts—I may hide the fact that I am a rogue driver.

Market imperfections (as if markets could be perfect!) explain part of the *illiquidity* of real estate. Since each property is so specific, potential buyers need time to assess it. Agents will help in the process but their cost is adding to the discount generated by the risk. The need to gather information incurs yet another cost: the idle period during which a property does not yield any revenue for lack of tenant. Financial institutions are not immune to these deficiencies. The French bank BNP Paribas kicked-off the subprime crisis in the summer of 2007, when it announced that it suspended three investment funds due to "a complete evaporation of liquidity". This jargon means that no one had a clue how much they were worth. Likewise, capital riskers have a hard time assessing the *fair price* of start-up companies. They cannot choose to be indolent and buy young businesses at market price because there simply is no market! Or rather, the market is a very thin one.

Buying *at-market* means yielding to the offer of the most competitive seller. In plain English, it means being lazy and trusting that such price will be reasonable. It sounds like an inconsiderate leap of faith. But let's remember that we do this dozens of times a day. You did not challenge the price of your last cappuccino (though it did seem pricey for a shot of coffee and some milk). If anything, buying at-market is the norm. This indolence is rational because the cost of investigating the fair price of each item bought and sold would be enormous. Anyone who's spent more than a week in a location where bargaining is the norm will acknowledge it. What a drain of energy!

As more people assess the same goods and information about past transactions flows freely, the *cost of laziness* goes down. There is a tautological aspect to the notion that a cappuccino should cost $5 because that's what everyone else is ready to pay for it. But from an individual perspective, this reasoning makes perfect sense. You are relying on other buyers to do the job. If this price was not fair, you reckon that shops selling it for $5 would have gone out of business. In other words, you are an information *free rider*.

For the system to work, participants must be numerous and diverse. Lazy *at-market* cappuccino buyers (such as office workers) must cohabit with hard hagglers (such as students). These participants collect information on cheaper shops and favour their business, thereby keeping prices under scrutiny. The information collection effort is not free and it benefits everyone else. So in theory, no one would do it. But the reason for which hagglers carry on is because it allows them to pay slightly less than the lazy buyers. This ecosystem illustrates the coexistence of *passive* and *active* investors on the stock market. Just replace students in our cappuccino illustration with hedge funds and high frequency trading firms.

In the housing market case, each good is unique. Moreover, there are few recent transactions. The only information available is derived from seemingly "comparable" homes that were bought and sold. In this system, lazily transacting *at-market* is expensive! Conversely, the reward for good bargains is high. If a flat with defects looks similar to one that has none, the cost of investigating is justified by the expected reward. Whenever laziness and haste are expensive, the market is *illiquid*. For venture capitalists, the reward for assessing *lemons* from *oranges* is extremely high. It comes to distinguishing the next tech giant from two teenagers playing in a garage! Again, it is the lack of information that explains why some markets penalize indolence more than others. If successful startups were easy to spot, they would be expensive from day one. And the reward expected from investing in them would vanish.

On the other hand, well-established businesses listed on an exchange are *liquid*. They are bought and sold in shares that are *homogeneous*. One share of Apple is identical to another. Like the currency market—where a pound is equivalent to another pound—it means that information flows into the system. People still disagree on the fair price. Otherwise, there wouldn't be a single transaction! But the point is that enough people are spending energy figuring it out for the "laziness tax" to stay low. Buying an Apple share at the price offered by the most competitive seller will not be unreasonably expensive given the current information. There are enough sellers to ensure that the most aggressive of the lot is offering a good price. It might eventually emerge that the marketplace as a whole was vastly overestimating the company's value. But this is a different matter. We are talking about *transaction cost*. Contrary to conventional wisdom, lack of expertise costs more when buying a flat than a stock index.

Selling a bedroom

Liquidity should make financial assets attractive. The ability to reverse a saving decision at low cost is a desirable feature. When confronted with unexpected circumstances, an arbitrary portion of the assets may be sold promptly at a reasonable price. If anything, this flexibility allows us to invest more because the necessary "safety cushion" can be reduced. Just as companies optimize their treasury by lending and borrowing overnight, people can use liquid assets to ensure that their money is put to work. The monthly repayment of a mortgage over the next three decades is incomparably more rigid! Choose one that is too close to your disposable income and you incur immense risk. This is why banks require a large buffer. What if my job situation was to change over the course of the mortgage? If it changes for the worse, foreclosure looms. If it changes for the better, the repayment rate may be too slow.

Despite all of this, liquidity is not typically perceived as attractive. As Barry Schwartz points out in *The Paradox of Choice*, people do not necessarily aspire to have extra freedom. A mortgage, with its asset and rate of reimbursement, is a one-off decision with enormous impact that stretches over a lifetime. And yet, it is perceived as more bearable than a series of small discretionary decisions. With financial investment, wrong decisions are easily noticeable. On the other hand, someone buying the wrong house in the wrong neighbourhood can choose to ignore it for decades. Systematic investing is one way to mitigate the psychological impact of regrets. As previously mentioned, people tend to pick their stocks and time the market. Not only is it bad from a risk-return perspective, it is an open door to regrets.

Saving is a tedious and painful process, which makes tying one's own hands attractive. The rigidity of real-estate investment is a powerful *commitment device* (like an expensive gym membership). One has no choice but to repay the mortgage at the pre-established rate. When facing unexpected expenses, it forces the consumption level to be the variable of adjustment. "With that new job paying less and the on-going monthly payments for the house, there will be no traveling this year." The rigid approach is appealing. It resembles the deficit constraint that European countries imposed on themselves. But these rules are only self-pleasing before the storm hits. Are you sure that your future self will find it preferable? Tying your hands is always done at a cost. The cancelled holidays might have been splendid. What if, in ten years, quality time with loved ones becomes more valuable to you than the extra bedroom?

The *divisibility* of financial instruments also constitutes a risk-mitigation device. When investors build exposure through decades of (patient) saving, they protect themselves against *point-of-entry risk*. Even when an asset is held for a long period, the final return is very sensitive to the time of entry and exit. If a large investment is made right before a market crash, it can be disastrous. Those who bought a house in the wrong locations shortly before the 2008 crisis have experienced it. The same happens when selling right before a price surge. A way to alleviate *point-of-entry risk* would be to buy and sell the house by small pieces, one square foot at a time. You lost your job? The children left the house? Sell a bedroom! This is fiction in the physical world but a cakewalk in the financial one.

Mobile me

The sensual pleasure derived from beautiful things is undeniable. Oscar Wilde found it "harder and harder every day to live up to [his] blue china." As he remarked, beauty does not require any form of justification. In this sense, it may be deeper than abstractions. Beautiful houses, cars and jewellery are appealing. In fact, our point is not to deny their importance! It is simply to observe that they make terrible assets. Possessing none of these things does not prevent us from enjoying their appearance.

In the tedious process of storing one's hard work into savings, the quest for social status and signalling is an expensive one. Entering a place and being able to call it "home" is pleasing. But it shouldn't lead us to disregard the cost of this gratification. Wear and tear, notarial fees and the various recurring expenses that come with physical possession are easily underestimated. Not to mention the price paid in the form of time. Human beings typically underestimate cost in most decisions. Surely an optimist trait that served us well from an evolutionary perspective.

The instinctive do-it-yourself approach is highly inefficient. Some enjoy the process of storing jewellery in a safe (and check every night that it is still there). Others point at a studio flat they rent out and proudly explain that they own it. The way of life that this author favours is different. Time, freedom and peace of mind score higher. In the age of cloud services, low maintenance is the true luxury.

Running a business incurs numerous costs and tasks that demand retribution. (These are called jobs.) By netting them from the value returned to capital owners, financial assets deliver a form of "net-of-trouble" return. Transaction costs, management fees and custody services must be paid for. Holding shares or bonds on someone's behalf requires a complex chain of services that have a price tag. But thanks to technology and vast economies of scale, these costs bear no comparison with the maintenance of physical assets. They have been dramatically reduced over the last few decades.

The freedom gained from dematerialized wealth does not only consist in extra time. It consists in valuable *mobility*. When everything you own fits into your identity (through the social protocol of entitlement), mobility is total. And it is way more than a hype concept for tech-savvy millennials. With no more lifetime jobs and women's enrolment in the workforce, it is a serious economic matter. Homeownership acts as a drag on mobility due to the low liquidity of real estate. It explains a large share of unemployment, as homes become a liability in locations where the job market is fickle.

Less Stuff, More Wealth

The process of innovation isn't linear. Companies come up with new products every year. They try their best to convince us that these are new. The truth is that improvement is marginal at best. And suddenly, a big leap, like the smartphone, occurs—a leap that allows more innovations to flourish around it. The reason why they come up once in a while is an open question. The most accepted theory is that they are made possible by *clusters of innovation*. Much like a perfect storm (but in a good way), several parallel technologies mature to a degree where they allow for more than the sum of their parts. Smartphones would not have been possible without better batteries and touch screens.

The Austrian economist Joseph Schumpeter is the father of this concept. He argues that clusters of innovation are at the core of economic cycles. The steam engine and the Electricity Age are classic examples of disruptive technologies around which new cycles began. Intriguingly, economists are still debating whether the computer was a defining technology of the same magnitude. By crunching productivity numbers (economists love productivity), many argue that it isn't. As the American economist Robert Solow famously noted in a 1987 quip, "you can see the computer age everywhere but in the productivity statistics!" A transformation as recent as this one is hard to assess. It might be that the metrics we use don't fully capture the sort of value these technologies deliver.

The point we make here is that several technologies have matured in a way that should let you rethink *savings* and *investment*. Beyond that, it should let us rethink *ownership* and *consumption*. What seems like a theoretical consideration is very practical: embracing that the things you own may never materialize to the naked eye. The maturing of *cloud services* is leading the emergence of what is called the *sharing economy*. The disappearance of material possession is gaining momentum. The 20th century definition of what constituted the *good life* (a house, a car, a TV and a docile wife) is being turned on its head. Consumption substitutes *access* for *possession*. The same process can apply to the wealth we tediously accumulate. This extra step has the potential to greatly improve life. So let's jump!

The Sharing Economy

"In 2015, Uber, the world's largest taxi company owns no vehicles. Facebook, the world's most popular media owner, creates no content. Alibaba, the most valuable retailer, has no inventory. Airbnb, the world's largest accommodation provider, owns no real estate." –Tom Goodwin

The sharing of production has been the big story since the Industrial Revolution. Modern economics starts with Adam Smith and the understanding of a key phenomenon: *division of labour*. Nearly three centuries later, we still live in this world. A production process based on few individuals (craftsmanship) was replaced by complex organisations involving hundreds of people. Progress was built around structures that surpass the scale of the individual. (Sometimes for the worse.) In this world, no single person can fully comprehend the production process in its entirety, let alone achieve it.

Vast amounts of capital and the *scientific management of labour* (also known as Taylorism) deepened the process. Immense productivity gains were made possible by the division of labour. Pushing this model came with its own demons, like the brutal working conditions of 19th century England (which gave birth to Marxism). Taking the individual out of the equation came at a cost. However "inefficient", craftsmanship had its virtues. Division of labour is not always compatible with the search for personal fulfilment, meaning and creativity (with all due respect to Wal-Mart and Starbucks).

David Graeber's "bullshit jobs" movement is the contemporary version of this thesis. An anthropologist at the London School of Economics, he argues that most of today's managerial, commercial and service jobs have turned into meaningless employment. The concern is valid. But it tends to exaggerate the fulfilment that the old system offered. Let's face it, most jobs aren't that interesting and never have been. If anything, there are more opportunities than ever before to turn that around for those who are brave enough and care enough. Not everyone is willing to pay the price that a fulfilling occupation demands. It takes hardship and a tremendous amount of work and faith. The paternalistic economy that told you what to do is dead. It is painful in some ways, but mostly a positive thing. Because, guess what, the world isn't waiting for you. If you think you deserve better, it is for you to demonstrate it. No matter how imperfect and unfair, Western societies offer options. It's called freedom and it ain't a walk in the park.

There is a vast difference between a job that doesn't offer straightforward meaning and one that is useless. Craftsmanship gives control to the individual over the whole production process. But there is a reason why it vanished in so many activities: its inefficiency. A great illustration of this is an experiment made by designer Thomas Thwaites. Intrigued by the complexity of the most trivial objects of daily life, he tried to replicate the equivalent of the cheapest toaster he could find. He decided he would build a similar one from scratch, using only raw materials and without resorting to any industrial input. He chose a £3.90 model that someone on the minimum wage would afford with half-an-hour of work. Making the same toaster from scratch took this resourceful man a full year. Undeniably, his version –if somewhat charming- was rubbish and unable to toast a slice of bread. It actually burst in flames as he plugged it in front of an audience. For the anecdote, it sold as a piece of art for $20,000. We live in funny times.

The story emphasizes the extraordinary accomplishment of the Industrial Revolution. Whether we are at home, on the street or in an office, the most trivial things surrounding us are packed with knowledge and technology. Individually building the things we consume (travels, meals, films, staplers) would be impossible even for the brightest minds. And we all take it for granted. It is as if we were collectively smart and individually dumb. The point is that we have become highly dependent on each other, in a complex system that overwhelms our understanding.

If this process transformed production dramatically, it hasn't altered consumption as much. Material possession of the goods we consume is still the norm. In the 20th century, services grew as a share of the economy. But their nature was basically unchanged. They included "anything that cannot exist as a good" (haircuts, shows, lectures). Thanks to the Information Age, we are finally cracking it. Our ability to process data is turning things that could only exist as possessions into services.

Sharing Economy, *Rental Economy*, *Collaborative Consumption*, *Access Economy*... These concepts capture different aspects of the *division of consumption*. They all have something in common. They depict a world in which capital never sleeps; a world in which idle resources are utilised as long as someone somewhere needs them. Empty apartments (AirBnb), underused cars (BlaBlaCar), idle lab facilities (Science Exchange), personal music collections (Spotify) and bulky encyclopaedias (Wikipedia) are becoming a thing of the past.

Lack of information—or the high cost of

gathering it, which is pretty much the same thing—was the major impediment. A *cluster of innovations* (cheap communication, data processing and storage) makes the leap possible. Material possession is obsolete simply because it is inefficient. This is good news for the consumer as much as it is for the environment. After all, this is about minimizing waste! The situation is unsettling for traditional producers. The eventual disappearance of employment as an institution is also an open question. We aren't there yet. The company as it exists is not fundamentally threatened by this transformation.

By using the new platforms, one can carry on owning an apartment while avoiding some of the ills of traditional possession (low mobility, leaving it empty during long absences). These landlords still own their apartment. But they do it very much in the same way a small business owns capital: striving to maximise its use. Tenants renting a room are turning into one-person businesses that do not speak their name. Likewise, *crowdfunding* turns households into bankers. It isn't so much that corporations increasingly run our lives, as it is our lives that increasingly run like corporations. *Non-exclusive access* is the key principle.

Possession and exclusivity are still relevant for many of the goods we consume. Why would anyone lend a fork? Though it is idle capital when it rests in its drawer, it is arguably far from a waste. The logistics behind a fork-sharing platform would totally outweigh the gains! The cheap value of the fork and its low storage cost does not justify the hassle. In this case, possession is the efficient scheme. But this model is losing ground. Some goods that belonged to the fork category (cars, flats, music collections) are falling out of it. Economies of scales used to be the privilege of large organisations. Technology brings it into your kitchen. In return for commission, intermediaries remove the heavy fixed costs and *barriers of entry* for small producers (private drivers, software developers, artists…).

Big data in the cloud

To get a general understanding of anything, a common mistake is to ask the expert. Experts are terrible at seeing the big picture, precisely because they lack distance with their subject. Market professionals are no exception. Having their nose on charts all day long, they get the intuition that equity valuation goes up as much as it goes down. An average 0.02% daily increase is imperceptible when prices swing up and down several percent. Thus, they tend to favour brick and mortar. The shoemaker's son always goes barefoot.

Likewise, try asking tech-savvies their opinion on the concepts of *Big Data* and *Cloud Computing*. I'd be surprised if you can trigger any excitement. They would barely accept the concept of Big Data and tell you that Cloud Computing has been around for decades. Technically, they are right. (That's why they are "technical" people.) The point is that Big Data and Cloud Computing are not technical concepts. They describe a paradigm. After all, the email—probably the first tangible intrusion of the Internet in our lives—was already a cloud service. A degree of maturity coupled with advances in other fields is what triggers a rupture. Innovations cluster to a point where something drastically new emerges. The challenge lies in identifying the cycle.

Contrary to what the name suggests, Big Data does not relate to any specific threshold. "Big" is a moving target in the history of our ability to store and process information. An instructive read on the topic is Viktor Mayer-Schnönberger and Kenneth Cukier's *Big Data: A Revolution that Will Transform how We Live, Work and Think.* According to the authors, Big Data can be defined by three major shifts. The first is the ability to deal with information without compromising with smaller samples. This aspect is disorienting for statisticians.

The second shift is the ability to cope with messy datasets. The concept of *unstructured data* was exposed earlier with news and social media-screening algorithms. Their objective is to process information that has not been "neatly organized in a table". Think about the way a self-driving car must process live recordings of its environment. We fail to appreciate how early in its infancy this ability is for machines. Tables and databases are the playgrounds in which our baby computers feel comfortable. The real world is still too complex for them.

The third and most intriguing aspect of Big Data is putting correlation at the centre, thereby abandoning the quest for "true" causality. It means that machines do not need to "be smart" in order to "act smart". A machine may interpret the meaning of a text not because it can "understand" it in the human sense but because it can recoup it with an enormous database that contains likewise formulations. This principle is the base for most of today's best-performing translation algorithms. Remember that *artificial intelligence* is not about making machines "intelligent". We don't really know what this would mean. It is about making them exhibit intelligent behaviour (the so-called Turing test).

The reign of *correlation* over *causation* is the triumph of *what* over *why*. Intuition becomes obsolete because the search for a valid base hypothesis is abandoned. When resources allow you to try all possible combinations, the gain from looking in the right direction becomes small. Brute-force capacity and computing power can do without the subtlety and elegance that previous approaches were forced to invent. But there is a justice in this world. Applied bluntly, these approaches can yield all sorts of fallacies. Brute force works. But state-of-the-art technology requires creativity. The fantasy that we finally have enough storage and processing power to solve any problem is an old chimera that has proved illusory. The goals that technology sets for itself shift like a horizon.

Algorithms and FinTech

What has this to do with personal finance? The growing usage of algorithms pushes the cost of complexity down. Or rather, the hierarchy of the things considered complex (and therefore expensive) is being turned on its head. Processing a $10,000 order to the stock market based on a systematic logic implemented by computers costs less than a haircut or a lunch at the local pub. Another way to look at it is to say that the haircut and the lunch have become more complex!

Financial markets have gone electronic. From noisy pits (only shown on TV to please journalists), they have turned into silent data centres scattered around the world. Trading floors are not the centralised physical location they used to be. The Chicago Mercantile Exchange, which processes more than 10 million contracts a day, estimates that 88% of them were traded electronically in the second quarter of 2015. A robot waiter is longer down the road than an algorithm that replaces your accountant! We still need experts to focus on complex problems. We still need art. But most of our useful-yet-repetitive routines can be automated.

This causes what economists call the *polarization of the job market*. People who conceive and design are in great demand, as well as those whose job is hard to automate. The middle range (industrial or administrative work that require some training) is an easier target for machines. A fair share of the occupations considered "low skilled"—like taking care of an elderly person—is very hard to mechanize. (No matter how hard the Japanese try.) This polarization fosters a concerning income gap. Isn't the middle class what holds society together?

There are reasons to remain optimistic. First, the process of increased productivity is desirable because it makes society better off as a whole. There are ways to redistribute the fruits from these gains. More importantly, automation redefines the *middle ground* more than it annihilates it. Due to the absence of productivity gains, low-skilled tasks become relatively more expensive. We could imagine a world in which an auto costs the price of a haircut (or a haircut the price of an auto, if you are a glass-half-empty kind of person). It seems like madness. But who would have thought 30 years ago that a computer would cost the price of a nice dinner in town?

Thanks to the growth of algorithms, sophisticated investment approaches have become cheap (and therefore, you might argue, less sophisticated). A large number of jobs are becoming irrelevant. The software-reliant ecosystem that emerges along big banks and within them is called *FinTech*. (Oddly, no one grieves over to the extinction of the banker.) Once able to charge hefty fees, asset managers now have to justify their existence. This is great news for consumers. Cheap cloud-investing services abound. They provide advanced services at a fraction of their original cost. Yearly fees for "the small guy" went down from several percentage points to a few hundredth of a percent! Low cost does not come at the expense of investor protection.

Steve Jobs famously described computers as a "bicycle for the mind". Technology puts complexity at the reach of anyone. Likewise, robot investment opens possibilities based on recent inventions (cheap data processing) as much as older ones (the public company). They rely on a Schumpeterian *cluster of innovations*. Mayer-Schnönberger and Cukier describe new data infrastructures as the 21st century equivalent of the Roman aqueducts or the Encyclopaedia. Money is already no more than information. The power to collect, convey and analyse cheaply and reliably changes saving just like it changed money itself.

The moment you press the "buy" button from the comfort of your sofa, a whole chain of trading, settlement and custody services takes place behind the scene. In the blink of an eye, you find yourself the owner of a tiny fraction of hundreds of businesses around the globe. In the process, you offer financing to a productive economy. This chain involves real people and painfully maintained machines from New York to Bangalore. Economies of scale, technology, rule of law and a myriad of patiently erected institutions are the only reason this magic is possible. In comparison, the acquisition of a house, with its lengthy procedure and overpaid solicitors is medieval!

The end of possession

The complexity of our financial system is overwhelming, even for so-called professionals like this author. And yet, it is nothing compared to "the ordinary business of life" (as Alfred Marshall defined the economy). When booking a plane ticket, we ignore the complex logistics that take place behind the scene. We press "buy". All we know is that it will get us from

A to B at a reasonable cost. The same should hold for investment. Making the most out of capital is not your job. Why add liabilities to a (complex enough) life? Running a successful business is an achievement that few can boast about. We admire entrepreneurs because most of us do not have the skills. Just like we love a good meal but aren't always able to cook one. For the same reason we delegate other aspects of our lives, let's delegate the usage of capital to those who do it best. These are company founders, managers and employees who wake up every morning to be part of an enterprise. Granted, they will make scores of mistakes. But will you really do better by yourself?

A mind-blowing aspect of developed economies is the extent to which we are willing to put our fate in the hands of total strangers. We often associate economic ties with personal interest and greed. We fail to appreciate the amount of trust necessary to give up the pursuit of self-sufficiency. Development is about deepening dependence on the group because it makes the individual better off. Today's urbanites not only can't survive in the wild, they increasingly don't know how to boil an egg! (Sometimes at the despair of this author.) As the system matures, best practices emerge in every single corner of our lives. The process behind renting and sharing is essentially the same as the one that lifted off standard of living over the last centuries.

Trust is precisely what finance is all about. Which is why financial assets are a natural extension of the model. We didn't wake up one day loving our neighbour. The protections erected have been critical in establishing trust. Countries with poor legal and judicial systems have a hard time developing. In today's world, one would rather lend money to a small company on the other side of the planet than to their brother-in-law! It is sad in some way. But is it? After all, there is nothing specific about your brother in law that would justify a favour (besides putting up with your sister). Our "community" simply becomes larger. Technology helps gather rich information on strangers. Mutual feedback and rating is used for information pooling (TripAdvisor), renting (Uber, Airbnb), sharing (BuzzCar) and social media (LinkedIn). In other words, the notion of a "total stranger" is fading.

In this reality, you still "own" things; but only indirectly. You do not own a car. It is idle and bulky. You own fractions of car manufacturers and rental companies; and rent from them occasionally. You do not own a secondary home. They are hard to maintain and underused. You own a fraction of many property developers, hotels and sharing platforms; and book from them from time to time. You do not even own a primary residence. They are illiquid and impede your mobility. You own a fraction of hundreds of well-run businesses; and use the proceeds to pay a rent.

We are the soldiers of a productivity-centric mammoth that is designed to extract the most out of resources (including ourselves). It has proved effective at raising living standards as long as we can keep it under check. Caught in schizophrenia, we are simultaneously the producer and the demanding consumer. So why not be the shareholder? They do not need to look like old white men who smoke cigars. In fact, the feared pension funds that are calling the shots on world markets are nothing else than the average person. Let professionals do the job and focus on your life. Young urban millennials are already embracing the *end of possession*. In the 20th century, owning a car, a home and a television was a sign of economic accomplishment. People increasingly realize that less stuff means less hassle. As the blogger and author Kevin Kelly put brilliantly, "access trumps ownership".

The sought-after car is the first victim of the wave. This author (like most men born in the 80s) used to fantasise about the day he could afford one. Twenty years later, I could not care less. Our generation still enjoys driving. (Something the next cohort will undoubtedly look down on.) But smoothly flying to a holiday location and renting a different vehicle each time is far more enjoyable! Cars driven for thousands of miles (typically by the tired father) only made sense because of the absence of a valid substitute. Today, we willingly embrace the alternative. The irony is that people have a hard time applying this mentality to the realm of saving.

We are the sum of our experiences, not the sum of our possessions. Let's not have a naive reading of this. If anything, it doesn't tell us that wealth isn't important. It simply means that wealth should be at the service of experiences—not at the service of things for their own sake. Material possession is nothing more than one way to obtain experiences. It is a terribly inefficient scheme that has served us well for lack of better options. Now is time to say goodbye.

The *end of possession* is a lifestyle. Resisting the call for social status is not easy. Being a landlord is the ultimate success signal in most countries. Social pressure is all around. But embracing material frugality does not mean turning into a monk! It does not even entail reducing consumption. Think of it as moving from the countryside to the city for a second time. Likewise, this way of life will not suit everyone. We will feel naked with nothing tangible to call our own, until we enjoy the breeze of freedom.

A practical guide

Finance is a tool. And now is the time to put theory into practice. If you hate the idea of trading and have no interest in markets, you are on the right track. The more you think you know, the more likely you are to take action. Do not. The following pages will teach you how to "do nothing efficiently". Delegate and focus on what you do best: live.

Better things to do

Institutional investors can be divided into three types. The first is the *activist investor*, who puts his nose into the circumstances of individual companies. He wants to influence the strategy and participate in the steering. Managers and founders abhor him. A prominent example is Carl Icahn. The *activist investor* suffers from bad press because he is not a likable character. He looks more like Gordon Gecko or Mitt Romney than Warren Buffet. And yet, he is a critical component of the system. He does the dirty job for other investors who have neither time nor patience for this. Without the *activist investor*, companies run the risk of becoming oversized leviathans with no sense of direction. They may be pre-empted by specific interest groups. The colourful activist is part of the balance of power that keeps decision-making democratic. He is a source of interesting stories for the financial press and keeps the show captivating.

The second type is the *active investor*. This kind is more discrete. He won't pick up his phone to complain or lobby the board of directors. In many ways, the *active investor* fits with the popular perception of the investor. He wants to *pick winners* and make smarter decisions than the average guy. His objective is to "beat the market". Buffet's Berkshire Hathaway is an example, though it sometimes falls in the first category (in a less aggressive style). When unhappy about the way things are done, the *active investor* votes with his feet. By doing so, he sends a strong message to companies' management. His feedback is more indirect since he owes no explanation. He walks away from problems instead of confronting them. Inferring that the active investor is a parasite would be unfair. He is part of the great information-gathering factory, working with less depth but more width. His actions participate in guiding the allocation of capital. Many retail investors are active investor wannabes—embodying the figure of the *day trader*. However, this inclination is a mistake. Watching numbers on a screen and reading financial news may impress your friends. But as we explained, successful stock picking requires resources and competences seldom found in a single individual. Even large players with immense artillery regularly fail.

Finally comes the *passive investor*. If you dislike the trader type (who doesn't?), this lazy bear appears likeable. He asks no questions. He buys and holds, under boom or bust. His opinion is that he has none. He has no view on the companies he owns, and no basis to question current market prices. He believes in wealth generation from businesses and has no plan to "beat the market". His objective is to be average. For this reason, the passive investor focuses on cost and diversification. If company A is *a priori* no better than company B, he is better off holding both. Passive funds replicate whole baskets rather than cherry picking. A fund that championed this approach is Vanguard. Trading becomes a cost to be minimized. The passive investor only transacts when he has to; for example if he needs cash or has some extra. He takes advantage of the hard work of the *activist* and the *active* investors. If one of the three types were a free rider, it would be this guy.

Now back to you. As a retail investor (*i.e.* a small guy), the passive approach is the only one you should consider. Not because it is smarter but because the other two are full-time occupations! Jobs receive compensation when done well. But remember, we are here to forget about finance and live our lives. Not to turn into day traders. Therefore, one approach is to pay a fee to the *active investor* and let him manage your hard-earned savings for you. This is the story that many traditional funds sell. Don't buy it.

The fees you pay will not cover the hypothetical extra return. Studies have shown that average active funds do not outperform passive ones after fees. Unless you are a big fish with strong bargaining power, this road is a chimera. All sorts of locking periods prevail and make the offering opaque. Chances are that you will overpay. The point is not to be judgmental. (There are honest bankers in this world!) But there is no gain to expect from running after such a complex model. In the realm of personal investment, simplicity is golden.

Passive investment services are cheaper than ever due to the rise of algorithms and FinTech. They are at the reach of anyone for less than 0.1% a year in management fees. Passive funds benefit from economies of scales on each level of the cost chain. These include trading, custody, unimaginable paper work, etc. Warren Buffet himself —the opposite of a passive investor— famously asked his wife to pour everything she owns into a fund that boringly tracks the U.S. market after his departure. Not because he doesn't trust her but because he believes that, all in all, she would be better off doing this. So would you.

The success of passive investing is not an unexplained anomaly that we happen to measure empirically. It has strong theoretical grounds. At its core is the concept of *market efficiency* explained in the previous part of this book. If you do not possess extra information, there is no point in participating in the beauty contest of businesses. Better focus on other aspects of the investment process, like saving and diversifying. Activist and active investors collect the value they produce in the form of the extra returns. But they will not share it with you for free. Just because "being active" can pay, it does not mean you should do it. It is merely a different occupation like, say, being a doctor. Rich academic research shows that retail investors are better off with passive index funds rather than micromanaging investment decisions. Not to mention the precious time saved for more interesting things!

Bogle and the low-cost model

The typical business is small and privately held. It is run and owned by its founder and does not employ a single person. Beyond a certain size, the status of *public company* becomes attractive, despite its constraints. It facilitates access to vast capital—the savings of the general public—through equity and debt markets. Though few in number, corporations with 500 employees or more produce more than half of private non-farm GDP in the United States. According to a 2010 estimate, only 14% of these large firms are listed on an exchange. But because the biggest ones typically are, public companies represent almost half of aggregate pre-tax profit. In other words, a fair share of the economy is open to the general public.

What finance commentators call "the market" is in fact a measurement tool that is no more than 120 years old: the index. Charles H. Dow unveiled the first one in 1896. At the time, it consisted of twelve stocks for which prices were simply averaged. This basic metric proved useful in assessing stock market moves. Because company sizes are so diverse, assigning the same weight to each of them was inappropriate. Today's indexes are therefore weighted by capitalization. A firm worth twice as much as another weighs twice as much.

The Standard & Poor's 90 was the first index to be computed daily. In 1946, IBM's punch card computer allowed the calculation to become hourly. The S&P index was expanded from the top 90 to the top 500 stocks. Nowadays, no country is complete without its flag, national dish and exotic-sounding market index. TOPIX, FOOTSIE, NASDAQ, CAC, DAX, NIFTY, BOVESPA are part of the landscape like well-known brands. The level of these indexes depends on the arbitrary value chosen on the day of their inception (typically 100). Indexes are expressed in "points" that bear no meaning besides the fact that they are proportional to capitalization (*i.e.* the price it would cost to buy the constituents at market prices). Because indexes have been around for a long time and valuations tend to increase over time, current values are typically in thousands of points.

As a passive investor, these indexes are what you're after. They offer great diversification. But remember, these are just metrics and there is no such thing as "buying" them. They are merely "replicated", which is far from trivial. Indexes potentially include hundreds of companies over several countries. Individuals investing $10 are therefore offering no more than fractions of a cent to the average firm. Stocks already allow you to buy a few dozen dollars worth of capital. But less than a cent is seriously pushing it! Transaction costs would absorb any of these trades. Which is why the *mutual fund* was invented. If I can find another thousand people willing to replicate the same index, why not pool our resources and share the resulting return? In other words, let's generate economies of scale. Risk is spread amongst investors without incurring spiralling costs.

The *mutual fund* emerged even earlier than the stock index. It can be traced back to 1774. A Dutch merchant named Adriaan van Ketwich theorised the principle of asset pooling. But actual take-off is very recent. It didn't happen until the end of the 19th century in Great Britain and France. In 1907, the Alexander Fund from Philadelphia was the first to feature regular issues and to allow investors to withdraw assets on demand. Two of the most prominent funds in 1928 are names that are still well known today: State Street Investors and the Wellington Fund. Even these "modern" funds were unaffordable for the general public due to expensive entry tickets. They were all *active* and charged their services handsomely. Modern portfolio theory only came around in 1952 with Harry Markowitz. At a time when nuclear fission was already well understood, academia had given little thought to diversification and the optimal way to combine assets.

The Wells Fargo Bank established the first index fund as recently as 1971. Four years later, John Clifton Bogle funded the Vanguard Group on the advocacy for passive index tracking. He insisted on its superiority over traditional actively managed mutual funds once fees were accounted for. "Jack" Bogle put his ideas into practice and funded the first low-cost passive index fund in 1976. The story goes that a Newsweek column from the economist Paul Samuelson acted as a trigger. The approach was received with scepticism. But after a difficult start,

Vanguard became the largest mutual fund in the 1990s. Bogle's book, *Common Sense on Mutual Funds: New Imperatives for the Intelligent Investor* was a bestseller.

In *The Arithmetic of 'All-In' Investment Expenses (2014)*, Bogle estimates that the yearly cost of active management is still around 2.7 percentage points. The figure is significant because long-term real returns on American equities have been approximately 6.5%. Moreover, the extra return from active management is not consistent over time. Funds that outperform one year struggle to maintain this edge over time. In this context, chasing low costs makes more sense than chasing great funds. Yet the message still finds its way with difficulty. People enter markets with hubris and bold objectives. The model proposed by passive management appears boring to the general public. Understandably, part of the asset management world perceives it as a threat to the existing business model. It takes bold new entrants like Bogle and today's FinTech firms to trim margins.

Heroes of modern finance aren't as sexy as their Silicon Valley counterparts. But their impact on our lives looms just as large. As of September 2014, Vanguard managed around U.S.$3 trillion. It was not far behind the largest of all, Blackrock, which managed close to U.S.$5 trillion. The numbers look daunting; but remember that World Inc.'s production in a single year (global GDP) is worth more than U.S.$70 trillion! The push for low-cost investment is still recent. A trend toward *smart beta* has emerged. It aims at improving a better profile than passive tracking by deviating from the index. Nonetheless, the case for simple index replication is strong for small investors facing high fees in the active space.

The ETF revolution

What was considered cheap in the 1970s wouldn't qualify today. *Exchange-traded funds* (ETFs) are the most recent step towards liquid, affordable and transparent index tracking. Like most great ideas, it is simple. Unless the underlying asset prevents it, investors should be allowed to enter and exit cheaply. Since the shares constituting indexes are typically liquid, so should the shares of the fund. Individual companies solved the liquidity problem by offering small and standardized portions of their capital (*i.e.* stocks). ETFs propose the same model with funds. They list shares that can be bought and sold like a common stock.

You may wonder why it took so long to come up with this product. Believe it or not, it requires actual technology. Exchange-traded funds could not exist without the emergence of trading algorithms and automation. Replicating indexes and making the market on these products is complex. Every time a U.S.$10 ETF is bought, a series of events follows. If it wasn't for a high level of computerisation, the service wouldn't be profitable and there would be no access for the individual investor. In other words, it would be 1975. Quotes are placed and adjusted real-time by affiliated market makers (at relevant prices and reasonable spreads). They must hedge their position, balance tracking error with transaction cost, reinvest dividends, abide by rules from different jurisdictions, follow up on custody services, etc.

As of 2009, there were more than 1,500 ETFs on U.S. exchanges alone. They provide access to indexes around the world from the comfort of the investor's domestic exchange. Foreign taxation, paperwork and other hassle are part of the service. Besides stocks, they track all sorts of underlying assets (bonds, commodities, currencies...). Some funds are even actively managed. Some are short, meaning that their value increases when markets go down and vice versa. Some are leveraged. Some are both. Some ETFs are physical (*i.e.* hold the underlying asset) while others are synthetic (*i.e.* use financial derivatives). In all cases, prudential regulation is tight and mandatory collateral protects the retail investor. Regulators are keen on keeping these products safe and transparent. ETFs are so efficient that even large asset managers use them.

In 2010, Vanguard's S&P 500 Index tracker had an expense ratio of 0.05% a year. It means that for U.S.$10k invested, the issuer charges an annual fee of U.S.$5 only. ETF providers have enough *asset under management* (AUM) to make the business model profitable. On top of this cost are custodian fees (usually waved or fixed at around U.S.$30 a year) for maintaining a securities account. Transaction fees are another expense, which is why you want to transact as seldom as possible (usually less than 0.25% with minimum floors). There are other technical considerations when trading ETFs like

147

implementation shortfall (the inability to perfectly capture the market price) and *tracking errors* (small differences between the underlying index and the performance of the fund). It sounds like a lot of costs, but they are tiny compared to active management. Not to mention the costs of homeownership! The march towards low-cost products is unstoppable. According to the Boston Consulting Group, ETFs made up half of all 2014 fund flows. They are expected to attract 35% of cumulative net flows between 2015 and 2018.

Getting started

No matter how simple, trading ETFs directly isn't for everyone. The process is a child's play compared to buying and selling an apartment. But it takes a little training. The goal is to be smart about your money while wasting little energy. A variety of "automated wealth managers" is emerging within FinTech. They take care of the process in return for low annual fees (typically 0.25% of assets). Betterment, Wealthfront, Personal Capital, Fund Advisor and Nutmeg are examples.

Their business model is simple. They rely on automation, ETFs and economies of scale. You could undoubtedly do it yourself. Shares are bought and sold as you add and retrieve money from the account. But if you are unfamiliar with financial markets—and uninterested in learning—their service may be just what you need. For U.S.$100k invested, it costs no more than a few hundred dollars each year to delegate allocation, trading and rebalancing. Such *robo-advisors* (also called *algo funds*) are cheap. These companies won't be profitable until they manage tens of billions of dollars. As of February 2015, the five of them combined managed no more than U.S.$5 billion of assets. Their clients are tech-savvy millennials with no sympathy for Wall Street and no trust for traditional banking services, perceived as inefficient and opaque. Never mind that these start-ups are the spiritual offspring of Vanguard as much as the Silicon Valley. Let's briefly explain their service and how it can be replicated.

Allocation is the process by which the fund decides how much should be invested into each asset class according to age and risk appetite. This isn't rocket science. (Even rocket science isn't rocket science.) Someone who needs the money "soon"—say, close to retirement—should hold stable assets like bonds. The volatility of stock markets would add risk without much benefit because the position won't be held for long anyway. Conversely, a young investor should pour money into riskier equity funds. Not because young people live dangerously but because risks are mitigated over time. Good and bad years will average out, leaving the investor with a return rate closer to the expectation of equity indexes. The long-term real yearly return from American equities has been 6.45%. At this rate, an amount of money would almost double in 10 years. Over 30 years, it would increase 6 to 7 fold and the chances of ending up in negative territory is minuscule. Based on the Dow Jones Industrial Average since 1900, the worst 20-year period was the one beginning in 1928. Even then—through the Great Depression and the war—it was still positive and equivalent to 2.5% a year. Obviously, the past is the past. But these metrics give an idea of the difference between long-term and short-term risk. As one grows older, wise allocation shifts more money to safer assets. (Being young and wise is not very wise!) If you shudder at the mere thought of losing some hard-earned money on markets, you might invest less in equities from the very beginning. Needless to say, diversification is a must.

Trading is seemingly the most exciting part. And yet—if done properly—it ought to be the most boring. Bear in mind that *good trading is little trading*. For mortals, buying and selling will never be a revenue generator. It only represents a cost. I repeat, a cost. What we are after is the exposure (holding the assets). The process of trading is nothing more than a necessary evil. It is friction in the process of investing. This friction is greatly reduced by the liquidity of markets. But all in all, you should consider that entering or exiting a position trims as much as 1% off the notional. These costs include fees, stamp duties and adverse market effects. All you need is a brokerage account, and most of them will offer low trading fees. Services like Interactive Brokers are more competitive. But the truth is that you will trade very little anyway. What you are after is simplicity and access. A securities account linked to your existing bank account is therefore an option worth considering.

The third service that these platforms offer is *rebalancing*. Say that you decided three years ago to allocate half of your wealth into stocks and the other half into bonds. If stocks slid over this period, your allocation is now biased towards bonds. Instead of the initial 50/50, your stock exposure is now 40% of the portfolio. Next time you save, you may only buy stock funds in order to converge back to 50%. You may also sell bonds to maintain your target allocation. *Rebalancing* is a common task for any index tracker. ETF providers need to rebalance on a regular basis to ensure that their holdings replicate the underlying index weightings. These are technicalities you can ignore when investing through *algo funds*. But if you are willing to buy ETFs directly, it is preferable to hold as few as possible. Keeping your portfolio down to three different trackers maximum will ease the process. For example, an ETF that tracks all developed markets is preferable to one that tracks the United States plus one that tracks Europe. *Rebalancing* is expensive, especially when you do it yourself. Not only does it cost time (and we prefer time well spent). It also means more trading (and we don't like trading).

Once the one-off procedure of opening a brokerage account is completed, the door to financial markets opens up! A U.S. citizen can easily access equities listed on the New York Stock Exchange (NYSE). It is only one of the many exchanges on the planet. But this is where the magic of ETFs happens. Not only do they replicate large and diversified portfolios into one single stock. They do so across borders and asset classes. A MSCI World tracker will replicate 1,500+ equities over 23 developed countries. More exotic indexes like the MSCI Emerging Market will feature higher fees (~0.15% a year). So would ETFs that track bonds. But the business model is the same. The provider takes care of the *hassle* at a low cost. Another part of their revenue originates from what is called *market making*.

Market making is probably the financial activity we are most familiar with. Anyone who's had to exchange money for traveling has been exposed to it. Currency exchange agencies offer to buy U.S. dollar in return for a given amount of foreign currency. They are also happy to sell U.S. dollar for this currency—but at a higher price. The amount it costs to sell one dollar and buy it back immediately is called the *spread*. If the initial dollar shrinks to 95 cents in the process, the *spread* is 5%. This is how *market makers* make a living. It may feel like a rip-off (and sometimes is). But you are paying for a service. These agencies do not need to turn your currency into dollars. You are the one asking for it and all they offer you is a quote. The same goes with ETFs. But because the notional is higher, market makers offer narrow spreads. For liquid underlying assets, the spread is typically 0.1%. At any point in time during market hours, an ETF would quote a price at which it can be bought (say U.S.$10.02) and one at which it can be sold (say U.S.$10.01). If you were to buy one share of this fund and sell it immediately, it would cost 1 cent for U.S.$10 invested (hence 0.1% spread).

Keep it simple, keep it fun

Whether you choose to do it yourself or purchase the services of *algo fund* makes little difference. Both are cheap and efficient. They eventually leverage on the same investment vehicles. In terms of protection, the result is also similar. ETFs are designed and regulated to be retail products, which means that they abide by strict regulations. Assets are segregated and guaranteed by collateral in the case of synthetic replication. But those that track illiquid underlying assets like commodities or emerging markets pose extra risks. No investment is risk-free and market moves are the major component.

Building wealth is dealing with two separate problems: the *how* (saving) and the *what* (investment). We already know the answer to the first problem and we don't like it. More savings means more work. We often spend more energy figuring out *what* to do with the little money we set aside when we should really focus on *how* to make more. Homeownership is not only popular because it is wrongly perceived as safe. It is popular because it is wrongly perceived as fun! Investment methods, like the ones we exposed, are about spending less energy on the things for which we have no added value. Making complex investment decisions is like making your own bread. It most likely won't produce better results and will be done at the expense of immense efforts. Whether we like it or not, most of us are better at making money than managing it. And the good news is that asset management has become cheap—bread cheap.

The perception that saving more is necessarily tedious is mistaken. Renouncing possession and futile consumptions is thrilling. It brings a sentiment of freedom and easiness. More importantly, it does not entail frugality! By giving up the quest to own things, we can enjoy them better. (The same goes with people.) Autarky and independence from the rest of the world is the chimera that we pursue through possession. Not only is it illusory, it is expensive. The alternative we promote is fun and liberating. Like anything in life, it can only be achieved if we derive pleasure from it. Imagine walking the streets of a city with no more than a few hundred grams in your pockets. Imagine not worrying about scratches on your car. Imagine that no mortar obstructs your mobility. The only physical objects you possess are worthless. What you own is nowhere and all around you at the same time.

When this author bought equities for the first time, it wasn't for personal account. I was a 25-year old intern in an international investment bank. I had no particular sympathy for shareholders (and still don't). My job was to design trading algorithms and I had no interest in stock investment. By the time I first bought an ETF for myself, I had already overseen the trading of hundreds of billions of dollars of client assets. And yet, it felt intimidating. Clicking "buy" is a jump into a new identify. You put on the top hat of the capitalist (if only a small-time capitalist). You suddenly own the means of production in addition to your own labour force. (The Marxist upbringing surfaces.) In one click, you are sharing the fate of companies whose names are familiar. You are now on both sides of the fence. The modest notional amount doesn't diminish the feeling. You have *skin in the game*.

The best time to start investing is *today*. The best investment horizon is *forever*. Resist the urge to time markets. Forget about the short term. If you are in your 30s or 40s, your time horizon is several decades. You will have many *entry points* that mitigate the risk. Simply save more when you can. Shortly after buying, you will typically lose money *mark-to-market*. You will pay a *spread* and trade against participants who are more sophisticated. Think of it as jumping on a moving train. It hurts. But the jump is only a necessary step. You are here for the ride, the *exposure*. The best way to minimize regrets is to stick to a systematic approach: *buy when you can, sell when you need to*. Being systematic is not something humans do well. We like to react. We like to predict. This instinct is great in the wild. But this is not a jungle. Reacting is a terrible habit on financial markets, unless it becomes your full-time occupation. So forget about the noise. Buy these assets as if they were a home, a shelter—because this is precisely what they are.

A bumpy ride called life

Investing isn't a walk in the park. At the time of writing this book, this author has been putting money into passive diversified funds for several years. The track record so far is close to flat! And yet, not only am I persevering. I am asking you to join me. All you know is that the *average company* returns more than cash in the *long run*. Stock markets beat their current high *eventually*. But this can take time! You will have to hold onto your chair and watch some hard-work money disappear. Things will get worse before they get better.

Only when you have skin in the game will you know how you personally react to crashes. *Mark-to-market* is not for the faint-hearted. Witnessing your savings lose 20% of their value over a week is hard to take. Investing is about looking past that. If you cannot stomach losses, it is time to shut this book. Apologies for wasting your time. Most people focus too much on *sunk cost*. I urge you to become an *opportunity cost* animal. (*Sunk cost* is about what has been lost when *opportunity cost* is about what could be gained.) You will face regrets from time to time. Again, bear in mind that you had no way of knowing. Market falls are sudden and shocking. Their growth is silent and gradual.

Diversification and market efficiency are on your side. What seems like theoretical considerations becomes very practical. For example, this author has been a strong believer in emerging markets. Reaching financial puberty in the 2000s meant seeing the world economy through the prism of the BRICs (the booming economies of Brazil, Russia, India and China). They felt way more exciting than old Europe and the United States. My personal instinct would have been to favour emerging countries and invest a large share of my hard-work money in them.

My personal instinct—as well as yours for that

matter—is rubbish. I am glad I did not trust it in the first place. A diversified portfolio should track broad indexes with multiple countries, including emerging ones. But you must resist the agonizing temptation to *pick winners*. The same goes with cool Silicon Valley companies that you deeply admire. The fact that 3M may outperform Tesla over the next decade is hard to accept. But it is the reality of stock markets; a place where the obvious has been priced-in before you could move a finger. As you will find out on occasions, acknowledging the extent of your own ignorance is a precious edge.

We also tend to favour what is familiar. American people invest in American companies; French people in French ones. This bias is understandable, but outright irrational. Unless you have a reason to believe that you were born in a blessed land (something your officials would like you to think), why deny the benefit of foreign diversification? Unless it entails a high degree of political risk or some core access barrier, there is no reason to tying your hands. There is nothing noble about economic patriotism (at least in this author's view). Taking no particular view by tracking an index like the MSCI World—which includes all developed countries—is rational and simple. Studies have shown that too many options on a 401(k) retirement account leads people to diversify less. They typically buy a little bit of each fund and end up more exposed than by pooling everything into one single well-diversified fund. Too many choices paralyze investors and open the door to regrets.

Benign neglect is the best attitude because there is no action to undertake after each market move. So why wreck your nerves? Prices go up? No need to sell. They fall? No need to buy more or sell in a hurry. These moves tell nothing about the future. You may be tempted to frequently check the market value of your portfolio. Do not. Diversification is not sufficient to make the ride smooth. (Which is why stocks still offer attractive returns.) A certain amount of thrill is unavoidable. Expect your assets to increase or decrease by 1% every day, even under mild circumstances. Over a year, they would typically move within a 15% band, which is no small swing. When things go pear shaped, a brutal 10% drop is not uncommon. If a proper financial crisis hits, broad stock indexes may halve peak-to-trough!

On the flip side, risk does add some fun to the boring process of saving. And saving is what ultimately matters. This author is anything but a gambler. Casinos and horse races have no excitement to offer. As Nassim Nicholas Taleb rightly points out, they do not live in the world of randomness. Quite the opposite! Nothing is more predictable than a casino's profit over a given day. The odds are known and—guess what—they aren't in your favour. The house always wins. Businesses, on the other hand, live in the world of uncertainty. Time is on their side, because they use resources efficiently. Wise investment is about harvesting these favourable odds. If you are in your 30s, most of your saving lies ahead of you. Therefore, facing a depressed market in the beginning of your cycle is not a bad thing! The wealth-building phase will last for decades. So don't panic. Financial markets offer a bumpy ride, like life in general. But if managed carefully, they need not be the casinos most of us picture.

Don't be a dinosaur!

Taleb illustrates his concept of *Black Swan* with the catchphrase "Don't be a turkey!" His point is that most experts use the same methodology as Thanksgiving turkeys. Tomorrow is expected to look very much like yesterday. Therefore, they are unable to foresee their tragic ending. History-based models are great at predicting future patterns most of the time. Except when it matters. "Changes of regime" (as analysts like to call something they didn't see coming) are no accident. They are part of the scheme of things. The final slaughter is precisely what motivated the regular feeding of the Thanksgiving turkeys! Economic agents behave as if recent history will repeat itself. The assumption behind the *subprime mortgage crisis* was that home prices never drop dramatically on a large scale. The evidence supporting this belief was purely empirical: it had never happened since 1945. Never mind that there was no theoretical ground for this! Housing bubbles had burst before and there was no reason to consider a nation-wide drop impossible.

What the eyes can't see, sometimes the brain should. Urbain Le Verrier discovered Neptune in 1846 before it could actually be observed. Using mathematics and observations of the known planet

Uranus, he was able to deduce the existence of another celestial body. Likewise, the turkey example illustrates that both data and theory are essential. Companies offer better returns than brick and mortar *empirically*. Better resource management is what explains it *theoretically*. This paradigm offers no certitude. But good data supported by theory is all we have. Even hard science is nothing more than a set of *falsifiable assumptions* waiting to be proved wrong. Airplanes fly even though we could be mistaken about the way we explain it! The discrepancies between Uranus's orbit and the one predicted by gravity could have turned out to prove Newton's physics wrong.

My tribute to Taleb's "Don't be a turkey!" is "Don't be a dinosaur!" As an investor, you want to avoid *extinction*. Obviously, there is a vast difference between *losing a lot* and *losing it all*. Market storms are no problem as long as you survive them. During downturns, indexes go through purges that can erase more than half of their valuation. Whether the drop is short or long lasting, the point is to be alive for the following spring. For sophisticated investors, the risk of wiping assets out isn't the end of the world. Extinction can be temporary and part of a wider strategy. But it is psychologically devastating for us mortals. In other words, extinction is a harsh experience. *Losing it all* drives people away from stocks for good. Interestingly, *negative equity*—where a house is worth less than the outstanding mortgage—seems less traumatising.

Survival follows two simple rules: *no picking, no leveraging*. The case against stock picking (investing in a few selected companies) was made in previous chapters. You have no clue which ones are undervalued. Picking winners adds risk and cost for no potential extra return. More importantly, businesses go bankrupt. It is what they do best. Remember that an index is different in nature from a company. The whole differs from its parts. When *stock picking* keeps you at the mercy of the next storm, *diversification* keeps you at the mercy of the next nuclear war (hopefully some more constructive structural change). In his scenario, losing all your savings probably won't be your biggest problem.

The case against *leveraging* is less consensual. Leverage refers to any technique that amplifies gains and losses. Typically, it is achieved by borrowing funds to invest beyond the initial capital. Businesses are leveraged by nature since they issue debt. Plain stock ownership is therefore already exposed to a fair amount of leverage. Remember that a stock is a right on what is left after all other obligations have been honoured. If things go wrong, their value can be wiped out. But it won't turn negative. On stock markets, leverage is at the core of most crashes. Investors who borrowed are forced to sell in a hurry because the stocks they acquired are used as a collateral. When things go bad, they have no choice but to sell in order to honour *margin calls* (deposits covering potential losses). In this chain reaction, forced selling causes prices to fall further, triggering more forced selling. When the bottom is reached, highly exposed dinosaurs are annihilated. Prudent mammals and new entrants thrive through the next cycle.

Leverage (if you're still tempted) can be achieved in different ways, from direct borrowing to the use of financial derivatives. In all cases, the objective is to amplify moves. The assumption is that the interest on the debt is lower than the expected return on the asset. This is exactly what most people expect from a housing mortgage. Such schemes can be valid as long as the risk is well understood. In *Lyfecycle Investing*, Barry Nalebuff and Ian Ayres rightly point out that extinction is no big deal when it happens early on in the saving cycle. The following gains are likely to outweigh the initial loss. According to their computations, sticking to a strategy that includes some leveraging is optimal. Their advice is to gear up and gradually reduce leverage over the life cycle.

As appealing as it is, leverage is complex, unnerving and it requires a certain degree of sophistication. It requires the use of future contracts, margin trading or less transparent types of Exchange-Traded Funds. Going full stock index exposure at a young age is already more risk than what most of us can bear. *Life Cycle Investing* promotes leverage with reason. But people aren't cold optimizing machines. The added value is questionable considering the extra cost, stress and complexity. Plain index replication offers a fair amount of leverage embedded in each company while sheltering investors from outright extinction. The point is not to avoid shocks. We simply can't do that. The point is to survive them. Leverage necessitates expertise and nerves. We are after efficiency and peace of mind. Simplicity is sometimes preferable to the true optimal method.

Let's not die rich

The irony of saving is that we often overlook half of the story: *dissaving*. This phase is unpleasant because it relates to the prospect of our own death. And yet, as far as the *life cycle* is concerned, it ought to be the best half! No matter how enjoyable it is to watch your nest eggs grow, they have nothing to offer until they turn into consumption. After pursuing A by using B as a means for a lifetime, it is all too easy to forget that A ever existed. The whole point of this is to live better, not die rich.

When retirement comes, you are left with two options: leave something for your children or leave nothing at all. If you end up facing the luxury of this dilemma, your kids probably received a lot from you already. Chances are that they were raised in a stable environment and received an education. This *human capital* is worth way more than any direct donation. More help might even be detrimental to their sense of achievement. Don't be so selfish! (It works both ways. If you have been a bad parent, money probably won't buy back the damage caused.)

These are, of course, very personal views. Of all levies, the inheritance tax is probably the fairest and most economically efficient. Excessive accumulation of wealth from heritage is more damaging than that from entrepreneurship. Old money is the problem. Given the exorbitant benefits that one already receives from being raised in a privileged environment, outright transmission of wealth feels unjustified.

Whatever view you hold, the key is to implement it. Traditional forms of savings offer very little leeway. Imagine for a moment that you would like to enjoy every dime of your hard-work money before you go. How would you achieve this? Personal savings in the form of a house you live in are difficult to liquidate during your lifetime! When would you sell it? What would you do with the proceeds? For this reason, real estate mostly ends up being passed on, for better or worse. Retirement rights are a form of wealth that is consumed entirely by design. But can personal savings replicate that?

Financial instruments have the advantage of divisibility. They can be accumulated over time. The same is true on the way out. A stock or bond portfolio does not need to be liquidated in one shot. You may sell it gradually, according to needs. If the need is less than the return that the asset generates, this could carry on indefinitely. Since life is finite, preserving capital in this way is unnecessary. And yet, it is precisely what people do when living in a home they own! The implicit rent is the return. The house itself is the capital.

This scheme is not satisfactory. First, few of us can hope to accumulate enough wealth to live comfortably out of interests only. Moreover, it is not even desirable. Ending your life cash-poor and asset-rich (with a greedy offspring waiting for your demise) is suboptimal to say the least. Let's assume that your plan is to spend it all. Stocks and bonds are divisible but you (fortunately) do not know your end date. It is therefore impossible to gradually sell your capital. What a depressing countdown it would be!

Death is an old conundrum. But what we have here is nothing more than a *cash flow* problem. And—guess what—finance is all about cash flow problems. A future cash flow has a *present value*, which is why stocks and bonds are worth anything. When buying a financial instrument, we are willing to pay upfront in return for being entitled to a future cash flow. Things are identical here. You are willing to pay a lump sum (your accumulated capital) in return for a cash flow that is finite in time. It is very much like buying a bond. The only unknown is its maturity: the day you die.

This morbid financial contract already exists. It is called a *life annuity*. (Bankers rival politicians in inventing Orwellian euphemisms.) The issuer—typically an insurance company—makes a series of payments to the annuitant over their lifetime in exchange for a lump sum. The first traces of such contracts go back to Ulpian of Tyrian, a jurist under the Roman Empire. Mathematicians as prominent as Bernoulli, Gauss or Laplace, have found interest in computing its fair value. Modern finance has an answer. If the date of your death is a mystery, the expected lifespan of the millions of people who receive a pension is not. Life annuities now exist in all shapes and forms. They can be fixed (for stability lovers), variable (for inveterate gamblers), guaranteed (for sore losers) or joint (for the romantic types).

The traditional homeownership model does not offer such flexibility. By the time you wish to enter a life annuity, more of them will have been invented. And the fees they charge are bound to drop. In the meantime, expect a couple of fierce crises to hit. But finance itself will survive, even if it has to move from Wall Street to the Silicon Valley. So be a smart mammal and stay away from extinction. Now that you know that you don't need to know, it is time to forget finance and focus on what really matters. It is time to embrace the end of possession and enjoy an existence with less stuff and more wealth.

Table of Contents

FOREWORD **6**
OVERVIEW **10**
   THE DIVISION OF USAGE 10
   CLOUD INVESTMENT 12
DIE-HARD MENTALITY **16**
   HOME, SWEET HOME 19
      Brick and mortar..20
      Safe havens..22
      A place to stand and a lever...........................24
      Being an ostrich..25
      Walls all around..28
      The ownership paradox..................................30
      Financial equivalence......................................32
   O CAPITAL! MY CAPITAL! 34
      This is mine...34
      Asset goods versus good assets.....................37
      Most capital is immaterial..............................38
      You are your most valuable asset..................41
      The case for equities.......................................45
      Traveling light...48
   MYTHS WORTH BUSTING 50
      Time the market right....................................50
      A zero sum game..52
      Trading generates revenue............................53
      Pick the right horse..54
      Be prepared to lose it all................................55
THE ONLY THING WORTH OWNING **60**
   SOURCE OF WEALTH CREATION 61
      Meet the cash flow...62
      Buying versus renting.....................................65
      Businesses at the core....................................66
      The invention of the public company............67

    Why stock markets go up *72*
  ALL YOU NEED TO KNOW 77
    High Expectations *78*
    Diversification *82*
    Volatility (and why we abhor it) *85*
    The discrete virtues of patience *91*
    Anchoring and other oddities *95*
  MARKET EFFICIENCY 98
    The bus allegory *99*
    Evidence *101*
    Faster than its shadow *104*
    What it means for you *108*

SAVING IN THE DIGITAL AGE **111**
  DISCRETE VIRTUES 111
    Liquidity, mon amour *112*
    Selling a bedroom *116*
    Mobile me *119*
  LESS STUFF, MORE WEALTH 122
    The Sharing Economy *123*
    Big data in the cloud *128*
    Algorithms and FinTech *130*
    The end of possession *133*
  A PRACTICAL GUIDE 138
    Better things to do *138*
    Bogle and the low-cost model *142*
    The ETF revolution *146*
    Getting started *148*
    Keep it simple, keep it fun *153*
    A bumpy ride called life *155*
    Don't be a dinosaur! *159*
    Let's not die rich *163*

Printed in Great Britain
by Amazon